GLASGOW MUSEUMS
Seventeenth-century Costume

Glasgow Museums
Seventeenth-century Costume

Rebecca Quinton

Unicorn Press

First published in 2013 by Unicorn Press Ltd in association with Glasgow Museums

Unicorn Press Ltd
66 Charlotte Street, London W1T 4QE

www.unicornpress.org

All rights reserved. No part of this publication may be reproduced or transmitted in any form or by any means, electronic or mechanical, including photocopy, recording or any other information storage and retrieval system, without prior permission in writing from the publisher.

ISBN 978 1 906509 86 6 (paperback)

Also available as an e-book
  E-pub ISBN   978 1 906509 87 3
  E-mobi ISBN 978 1 906509 88 0

British Library Cataloguing in Publication Data
A catalogue record for this book is available from the British Library

Text copyright © 2013 CSG Glasgow Museums
Images copyright © 2013 CSG CIC Glasgow Museums and Libraries Collections unless otherwise acknowledged.
Images available from www.csgimages.org

Written by Rebecca Quinton
Designed by Nick Newton Design
Edited by Fiona MacLeod, with Vivien Hamilton and Helen Watkins

Printed in Singapore by Craftprint

Cover: Detail of fig. 45
Frontispiece: Detail of fig. 19
Page 14: Detail from *The Family of Sir Robert Vyner*, 1673 © National Portrait Gallery, London

Photographic Acknowledgements

Figs 5, 43, 46, 47, 51 © English Heritage
Figs 6, 7, 11, 12, 31, 63, 87 © National Portrait Gallery, London
Fig. 9 © Yale Center for British Art, Paul Mellon Fund USA / The Bridgeman Art Library
Fig.10 © Ham House Surrey, UK / The Stapleton Collection/ The Bridgeman Art Library
Fig. 15 © Folger Shakespeare Library, Washington DC, USA
Fig. 41 © Fashion Museum, Bath and North East Somerset Council / Lent by Mrs Bateman and Mr Porter / The Bridgeman Art Library
Fig. 42, 73 © Victoria and Albert Museum, London
Fig.59 © reproduced by kind permission of the Governors of George Heriot's Trust, Edinburgh
Fig. 64 © Fairleigh Dickinson University
Fig. 74 © Scottish National Portrait Gallery
Fig. 79 © The National Gallery, London

Contents

Foreword Dr Ellen McAdam, Head of Museums and Collections	6
Acknowledgements	7
Places to visit	7
The Camphill Fund	7
Seventeenth-century Costume in Glasgow Museums	9
The Seventeenth Century	15

THE COLLECTION

Jacobean Nightcaps	27
Jacobean Coifs	37
Blackwork	51
Embroidered Waistcoats	57
Embroidered Petticoat	67
Gloves	77
Falconry Accessories	83
Bags	97
Knitted Waistcoat	105
Items Associated with Charles II and Oliver Cromwell	111
Restoration Items	123
Late Seventeenth-century Accessories	133
Catalogue Information	137
Biographies of Collectors and Dealers	140
Glossary	141
Bibliography	142
Index	145

Foreword

This catalogue by Rebecca Quinton of the seventeenth-century costume in the collection of Glasgow Museums is the second in a planned series of catalogues raisonnés, the first having been Professor Peter Humfrey's magisterial work on the Italian paintings, published in 2012. The fact that this deals with so different a subject is an indication of the astonishing breadth and richness of Glasgow's collection.

Few objects tell us as much about the role of an individual in a society as their clothes. Status, age, sex, marital status, occupation, religion and political affiliations could all be encoded. Industrialization began a process of change that the mass production of very cheap clothes in the twenty-first century has taken much further. One of the effects has been the levelling out of most of the coded information. Young women of slender means on their nights out dress with the sophistication of celebrities. Office workers of all ages have adopted a dreary uniform of grey, black and navy blue. Except in very cold weather and at weddings, head coverings are virtually unknown.

How very different costume was in the seventeenth century, with the colours of its embroidery, the liquefaction of its silks, the stiffness of its brocades, the solidity of its good broadcloth, its yards of ribbon and braid and fine lace, its doublets and breeches and full skirts. No doubt these clothes were uncomfortable to wear and a nightmare to keep clean, but how brave and rich their appearance, and how many messages they convey about the wearers! One can forgive Charles II much – his mistresses, his foreign policy, his frivolity – but one cannot forgive him for being the progenitor of today's grey, black or navy blue business suit.

Dr Ellen McAdam, Head of Museums and Collections

Acknowledgements

I would like to extend special thanks to the following people for their assistance with this book: Liz Arthur, Chris Berry, Mary Duxbury, Ruth Gilbert, Christina Sebastian, Maureen Smith, Naomi Tarrant, the late William Wells, and David Wilcox.

Places to Visit

United Kingdom
Burrell Collection, Glasgow Museums, Glasgow
Victoria and Albert Museum, London
Museum of London, London
Fashion Museum, Bath
Gallery of Costume, Manchester

United States of America
Costume Institute, Metropolitan Museum of Art, New York
Museum of Fine Arts, Boston

Please remember that displays are subject to change, and you should check before travelling that the items you wish to see are on display.

The Camphill Fund

The Camphill Fund was established in 1984 to promote Glasgow Museums' costume and textiles collections. The Fund takes its name from Camphill House, an eighteenth-century house on the south side of Glasgow, where the collection was formerly housed.

Funds have been raised by holding events, such as fashion shows and masked balls, and from generous donations from the business sector. Money from the Fund has gone toward the conservation of the late sixteenth and early seventeenth-century hangings from Lochleven Castle, the provision of mannequins, exhibitions, and publications on the collection.

Today the collection is housed at Glasgow Museums Resource Centre and the Burrell Collection, Glasgow, where it is available for study and research.

And Thus without the Needle we may see,
We should without our Bibbs and Biggings be;
No shirts or smocks, our nakedness to hide,
No Garments gay, to make us magnifyde;
No Shadowes, Shapparoones, Caules, Bands, Ruffes, Cuffes
No Kerchieves, Qoufyes, Chin-clowtes or marry-Muffes,
No Cros-cloathes, Aprons, Hand-kerchiefs, or Falls,
No Table-cloathes for Parlours or for Halls.

John Taylor, 'In Praise of the Needle',
The Needle's Excellency, 1631

Seventeenth-century Costume in Glasgow Museums

Glasgow Museums has collected European costume and textiles since the late nineteenth century. The first items to be purchased were textiles produced by local manufacturers, including Turkey red and carpets. These were supplemented by lace and Italian brocaded silks acquired from the Glasgow International Exhibition in 1888 as well as individual purchases, such as a late seventeenth-century fan (fig. 1). Today the collection contains approximately 18,000 items dating from the medieval period to the present day. This book, the first in a series exploring the highlights of the collection, focuses on the seventeenth-century costume in Glasgow Museums. While this is a relatively small area of the collection, consisting of approximately 30 items, it is an important one that contains several items of international significance to the study of dress history.

Due to their age items of seventeenth-century dress rarely survive. Textiles in general were expensive and many items would have been reused or the cloth recycled until they became too fragile or too worn for further purpose. As a result the items that have survived to the present are often

Fig. 1: Fan, Dutch or Italian, about 1690–1700 (1883.32.bf)

This fan was one of the first items of European costume to be acquired when it was purchased in 1883. It is also the earliest of approximately 150 fans in the collection, the majority of which date to the nineteenth century.

Fig. 2: Detail of petticoat, British, about 1610–20 (29.314)

This petticoat panel is a very rare survivor. Historic textiles were often reused, sometimes to make interior furnishings, such as curtains or cushions. Whilst this panel was altered at a later date, the changes were relatively minimal.

the costly, high quality garments worn by members of the higher echelons of society: royalty, aristocracy and gentry. Pieces would have been given to relatives or to close personal servants as prerequisite gifts, such as happened to an early seventeenth-century petticoat given by Charles I (1600–49) to his Groom of the Bedchamber, William Levett (1625–93) (fig. 2). These subsequently passed down through generations, becoming treasured family heirlooms. Several items, especially small accessories, were collected by connoisseurs during the late nineteenth and twentieth centuries, their survival dependent on their intrinsic merit, the materials and techniques used, or an illustrious provenance or association.

Glasgow Museums' European Costume and Textiles collection developed during the twentieth century, primarily as a result of generous donations from the public and designers. Initially this created a fairly random and disparate collection of objects, but since the 1970s a more uniform approach to collecting has been undertaken. It is now possible to use the collection to trace the continuous development of European fashionable dress from the 1760s onwards. Earlier pieces in the collection cluster in periods or stand alone in isolation.

The majority of seventeenth-century costume in Glasgow Museums is in the Burrell Collection. Sir William Burrell (1861–1958), a wealthy Glaswegian shipping magnate, began collecting fine and decorative art as a young man in the late nineteenth century and continued his passion throughout his long life. His interests included paintings, medieval and Renaissance tapestries, sculpture and stained glass, and European, Islamic and Chinese ceramics and metalwork. In 1944 Sir William and his wife Constance, Lady Burrell, gifted their collection of approximately 6,000 items to the city of Glasgow, adding a further 2,000 pieces over the following 14 years until Sir William's death. Unusually, the Burrell Collection is not closed, as items are still purchased by the Trustees of Sir William's bequest to add to his original gift. Today his collection is housed in a purpose-built museum in Pollok Park, Glasgow, but during his lifetime many pieces were used to furnish Burrell's various rented and owned properties. After his purchase of Hutton Castle, near Berwick-upon-Tweed in the Scottish Borders, in 1916, the building was extensively refurbished in the country house style and decorated with many of his purchases (fig. 3). Burrell also lent items to museums, such as the Bowes Museum in County Durham, and to major

Fig. 3: Tower Sitting Room, Hutton Castle, 1940s or early 1950s

This photograph shows several embroideries framed and hung in Hutton Castle, including a late-seventeenth century stomacher (fig. 88) above the fireplace.

exhibitions, including the Glasgow International Exhibition in 1901.

Like other contemporary collectors, such as William Hesketh Lever, later Viscount Leverhume (1851–1925), whose collection is in the Lady Lever Art Gallery, Port Sunlight, and Judge Irwin Untermyer (1886–1973), who donated his collection to the Metropolitan Museum, New York, Burrell's interest in sixteenth- and seventeenth-century decorative art extended to textiles, especially needlework, resulting in the acquisition of approximately 300 items. Unsurprisingly this includes several examples of seventeenth-century costume, particularly from the early 1600s, when the fashion for embroidered garments and accessories was at its height. Alongside typical collectors' items, such as nightcaps and coifs, there are items of particular significance, including a group of falconry accessories that belonged to James VI of Scotland and I of England (1566–1625) (fig. 4). In contrast, costume from the

Fig. 4: Falconry accessories used by James VI and I, British, early seventeenth century (29.151.1–5)

According to his Purchase Book, Burrell paid £1,100 for this group of falconry accessories in 1934. It was his most expensive needlework purchase, costing more than several small tapestries and over three times the price of a pastel by Edgar Degas, which he had bought the previous year.

reign of Charles I and his French wife, Henrietta Maria (1609–69), was not collected by Burrell, as silk satins decorated with slashed or punched motifs were fashionable rather than embroidered textiles.

Sir William Burrell, in common with several early twentieth-century collectors, appears to have been interested in the aesthetic and technical aspect of an object more than its social history. The majority of his pieces were purchased directly from dealers or by them acting as an intermediary at auction. One of his key contacts for needlework was the antiques firm Frank Partridge & Son, who also acquired many items for both Lever and Untermyer. The disadvantage of Burrell buying his collection third-hand is that the provenance of many items was not documented; the agent or dealer rarely disclosed it and Burrell does not appear to have made further enquiries. The exception to this rule is where monarchy is associated. Like many others, Burrell was not averse to buying items that had a royal pedigree, often at a premium. There are two groups of accessories related to the period of the Civil Wars, the first said to have belonged to Charles II (1630–85), when Prince of Wales, and the second to Oliver Cromwell (1599–1658), both of which were probably acquired more because of their attributed history than their aesthetic quality.

This book focuses on the context and history of the examples in Glasgow Museums' collections, with individual or group entries arranged thematically in a loose date order rather than in a strict chronology. As often happens with object-based research, interesting discoveries have been made and some items have been re-classified. One such example discovered during conservation work undertaken in 1987 was that a small cushion had been made from a coif with its edges folded in (fig. 28). In other instances, where items are particularly rare and there are few, if any, comparative pieces, deductions made here may be shown in time to be incorrect when further evidence is discovered. It is hoped that by publishing the items in Glasgow Museums' collection, and thus enabling them to become better known alongside surviving garments, portraits and written sources in other collections, they can contribute to the wider understanding of seventeenth-century dress.

The Seventeenth Century

The clothing of an era is often a good reflection of the wealth of a nation and this is particularly true of the seventeenth century. The early 1600s was a period of peace and prosperity for Britain as a result of the Union of the Crowns in 1603, when James VI of Scotland inherited the English throne after the death of Elizabeth I (1533–1603); an event that is particularly remarkable for being one of the smoothest transitions between dynasties in British history. The subsequent harmony between the separate kingdoms and absence of a continental war allowed for two decades of growth. Merchants enjoyed new trading opportunities not only in Europe but also further afield, with the granting in 1600 of a Royal Charter to the Governor and Company of Merchants of London trading with the East Indies, later known as the East India Company. An influx of luxury goods, including lace, silk and dyes entered Britain, providing wealth for trade and commerce.

At the centre of fashionable life was the court of James Stuart, which moved from Edinburgh to London upon his accession. The king surrounded himself with handsome favourites, who, just as they had in his predecessor's reign, dressed flamboyantly to show their youth, wealth and importance. During a period of conspicuous consumption Jacobean courtiers dressed in overtly lavish embroidered garments, often worn layered and further embellished with jewels and intricate lace. Portrait painters of the period paid particular attention to these details, as shown in William Larkin's portrait, *Edward Sackville (1591–1652), 4th Earl of Dorset*, 1613 (fig. 5). The excellence of English embroidery was known throughout Europe. The intricately wrought ecclesiastic vestments embroidered in *Opus Anglicanum* (English work) that used techniques such as split stitch and *or nué* (shaded gold) had been highly regarded and were coveted both in England and on the continent during the late thirteenth and early fourteenth centuries. English embroidery continued to flourish, despite the dissolution of the monasteries at the order of Henry VIII (1491–1547) from 1536 to 1541 and subsequent Protestant Reformation under his son Edward VI (1537–53). Instead, the highly

Opposite Detail from fig. 11

developed professional skills used to decorate vestments and liturgical textiles for the church were utilized to embroider clothing and domestic furnishings for secular clients. In 1561 the earlier English Guild of Embroiderers was re-founded as the Broderers' Company, with apprenticeships normally lasting eight years. One of the best-known embroiderers of the seventeenth century was Edmund Harrison (1591–1667), warden of the Broderers' Company, who was commissioned to make items for James VI and I, Charles I and Charles II. Professional embroiderers in Scotland were members of the Incorporation of Tailors and supplied the Scottish parliamentary and law courts' robes in Edinburgh.

The use of needlework to decorate dress is particularly evident in the fashions of the first two decades of the seventeenth century. This is also the era that saw an increase in the trickle-down effect of fashion, with rich clothing worn not only by the aristocracy but also by the increasingly wealthy and aspirational mercantile and professional classes. In part this was due to James VI and I, who rescinded the medieval and Tudor sumptuary laws that had previously restricted the use of rich textiles and fur to clothing for the nobility only.

Initially, seventeenth-century women's fashions were slow to evolve as James VI and I's wife, Anne of Denmark (1574–1619), chose to dress conservatively, favouring the large French or wheel farthingales worn by Elizabeth I in the last two decades of her reign, as depicted in John de Critz the Elder's portrait, *Anne of Denmark*, about 1605–10 (fig. 6). Whilst not regarded as a leader of fashion, Anne was a great patron of the arts. This role had been restricted in Presbyterian Scotland but flourished in the livelier English court, resulting in support for playwrights such as William Shakespeare (1564–1616), as well as artists and architects, most notably Inigo Jones (1573–1652), who designed the Queen's House, Greenwich, for her.

Taste began to change after the accession of Charles I in 1625. Both he and his wife, Henrietta Maria, preferred what were thought to be the more sophisticated fashions of the French court. Whilst the clothing of this period is as sumptuous and expensive as the preceding era, the elaborately embroidered textiles of the Jacobean court were replaced by plainer-looking lustrous silk satins, as seen in the

Opposite **Fig. 5:** William Larkin, *Edward Sackville (1591–1652), 4th Earl of Dorset*, 1613. Oil on canvas, 206.6 × 122.6 cm. English Heritage, Kenwood House, Suffolk Collection, London

Edward Sackville's doublet, breeches and cloak are covered with expensive embroidery worked in silver and silver-gilt thread. His outfit is accessorized with a delicate linen cutwork band.

The Seventeenth Century 17

Opposite Fig. 6: John de Critz the Elder, *Anne of Denmark*, about 1605–10. Oil on canvas, 201.6 × 126.5 cm. National Portrait Gallery, London

Anne of Denmark's continued use of the French farthingale may have been politically motivated, allowing the new Queen Consort to retain a visual continuity with Elizabeth's style.

Fig. 7: Cornelis Janssens van Ceulen, *The Capel Family*, about 1640. Oil on canvas, 160 × 259 cm. National Portrait Gallery, London

As was customary until the late nineteenth century the children are dressed in the same fashions as their parents, Arthur Capel (1604–49), 1st Baron Capel, and his wife Elizabeth, Lady Capel (died 1661), in satin doublets and breeches or gowns with soft falling lace bands.

group portrait by Cornelius Janssens van Ceulen (also known as Cornelius Johnson), *The Capel family*, about 1640 (fig. 7). The line is softer, with the wider décolletages on women's gowns often covered with falling bands that drape over their shoulders, similar to those worn by the men. The best were made from expensive imported lace. However, Charles I not only copied the clothing, but also the absolutist monarchy favoured by the Bourbon kings of France, culminating in an 11-year period of personal rule without parliament from 1629–40. The subsequent Civil Wars in England, Scotland and Ireland had a marked effect on the state of the three kingdoms, but also on the countries' wealth. The historic view of dashing Cavaliers and sombrely dressed Roundheads is incorrect; in practice there were people on both sides who continued to wear flamboyant articles of dress alongside their military apparel, their allegiance on the field indicated by the colour of their sash alone. It was not until the creation of the New Model Army in 1645 that soldiers wore uniform dress. The Puritans' preference for black and plain linen collars and cuffs reflected their religious more than political beliefs. When others adopted Puritan-style dress during the Commonwealth it was not necessarily a cheaper alternative, as good quality black cloth could be costly and many portraits show that outfits were accessorized with extremely

Fig. 8: Cornelius Johnson, *Cornelia Veth*, 1644. Oil on canvas, 78.7 × 63.5 cm. Tate, London

The crisp whiteness of the kerchief edged with white lace is shown off by the pristine black of the silk velvet gown.

fine and expensive lace, as seen in Cornelius Johnson's painting, *Cornelia Veth*, about 1644 (fig. 8).

After the Restoration of Charles II in 1660 England and Scotland prospered through commerce, manufacturing and trade. The Revocation of the Edict of Nantes in 1685 removed the rights granted to French Protestants, known as Huguenots, by Henry IV of France (1553–1610) nearly a century earlier and resulted in many exiles settling in Britain. The Huguenots brought new skills and textile machinery to an already well-established native industry. Consumer confidence was high and the importation of luxury goods from the continent flourished, the latter to such an extent that the parliament in Westminster began to pass laws to protect the growing English industries.

During a period of increased prosperity clothing once more became an obvious means of displaying a person's wealth and social status. The 1660s saw the return of French influences to both men's and women's fashions as the new court of Charles II tried to emulate that of Louis XIV (1638–1715), the Sun King. This was particularly true for gentlemen, who wore short doublets that revealed their white linen shirts and wide-skirted petticoat breeches, all elaborately decorated with lace, braid and yards of ribbons, as seen in John Michael Wright, *Sir John Corbet of Adderley*, about 1676 (fig. 9). Charles II was an arbiter of taste, with what he wore quickly being copied by court and city alike. When he introduced a new type of men's wear its appearance was immediately recorded by the diarists of the period. Samuel Pepys (1633–1703), writing on 8 October 1666, includes the entry in his *Diary* '[t]he King hath yesterday in council declared his resolution of setting a fashion of clothe which he will never alter'. A week later on 15 October Pepys added:

> This day the King begins to put on his vest, and I did see several persons of the House of Lords and Commons too, great courtiers, who are in it; being a long cassocke close to the body, of black cloth, and pinked with white silke under it, and a coat over it, and the legs ruffled with black ribband like a pigeon's leg: and, upon the whole, I wish the King may keep it, for it is a very fine and handsome garment.

Pepys later writes that his own tailor delivered a 'vest' for him on 5 November. The vest is believed to have been

Fig. 9: John Michael Wright, *Sir John Corbet of Adderley*, about 1676. Oil on canvas, 127 × 101.6 cm. Yale Center for British Art, New Haven, Connecticut, USA

The robes of the High Sheriff of Shropshire worn by Sir John Corbet demonstrate the liberal use of braids and ribbons popular during this period.

Fig. 10: Hendrick Danckerts, *John Rose, the King's Gardener, presenting Charles II with a pineapple*, 1675. Oil on canvas, 96.6 × 114.5 cm. Ham House, The Stapleton Collection, London

Both Rose and Charles II are wearing thigh-length vests with lace cravats. Originally worn by Croatian mercenaries in France during the 1630s, cravats were first worn in England in the 1650s.

influenced by the cut and construction of Persian men's wear. Hendrick Danckerts, in his painting *John Rose, the King's Gardener, presenting Charles II with a pineapple*, shows the monarch wearing a later version of the vest (fig. 10). By the 1680s the garment, later known as a coat, would be worn over a waistcoat, becoming the dominant form of men's fashion throughout Europe for the next 150 years and the forerunner of the modern three-piece suit.

In contrast to the monarch, his wife Catherine of Braganza (1638–1705) had much less influence on women's fashion. Her early appearances at court wearing traditional Portuguese court dress over a wide farthingale were ridiculed by her contemporaries. She quickly adopted the French fashions worn by Charles II's mistresses and favourites that trickled down to the professional and trading classes. These

The Seventeenth Century 23

gowns were constructed with long, boned bodices and full skirts held out with petticoats rather than hoops, as worn by the young Bridget Hyde (1662–1734), later Duchess of Leeds, in John Michael Wright's portrait, *The Family of Sir Robert Vyner (1631–1688)*, 1673 (fig. 11). During the 1690s a new type of gown, known as a mantua, evolved from informal nightgowns, such as that worn by Mary, Lady Vyner (died 1674). These were loose-fitting open gowns with their bodices often fitted to a decorative v-shaped panel or stomacher and their long over-skirts folded up into the back to form a train, revealing the matching petticoat below. Like the men's suit, the three-piece female outfit – gown, stomacher and petticoat – would become the model of the eighteenth-century dress.

Fig. 11: John Michael Wright, *The Family of Sir Robert Vyner*, 1673. Oil on canvas, 114.8 × 195.6 cm. National Portrait Gallery, London

Whilst Sir Robert and Mary Vyner are dressed informally in nightgowns, the children are depicted in fashionable day wear. Bridget, Sir Robert's step-daughter, wears a long-waisted gown and their son, Charles (1666–88), wears the new vest trimmed with ribbons.

Chronology

1603 Death of Elizabeth I of England, accession of James VI of Scotland as James I of England

1605 Weavers in Glasgow incorporated by Seal of Cause

1616 Death of William Shakespeare

1619 Death of Anne of Denmark, consort of James VI and I

1620 Pilgrims leave Plymouth on the Mayflower

1625 Accession of Charles I; Charles I marries Henrietta Maria

1629 Charles I dissolves the English Parliament and begins 11 years of absolute rule

1631 English Act of Parliament permits the importation of chintz, embroideries, quilts and other items from the East Indies

1638 Solemn League and Covenant signed by Calvinists in Scotland

1641 Beginning of the Civil Wars in England, Scotland and Ireland

1649 Execution of Charles I; foundation of the English Commonwealth; Charles II proclaimed King of Scotland by the Covenanter Parliament

1653 Oliver Cromwell becomes Lord Protector

1658 Death of Oliver Cromwell; succeeded by his son Richard Cromwell

1660 Restoration of Charles II

1662 Marriage of Charles II to Catherine of Braganza

1666 Great Fire of London

1673 James, Duke of York, marries Mary of Modena

1675 English Act of Parliament bans French and Flemish lace

1677 Princess Mary, daughter of James, Duke of York, marries William of Orange

1685 Accession of James II of England and VII of Scotland

Revocation of the Edict of Nantes, French Protestants flee to England

1688 Glorious Revolution; James VII and II deposed and exiled
English Act of Parliament bans the exportation of un-dyed cloth in order to promote the English dye industry in competition with the Scottish dye industry

1689 Accession of William of Orange as William III of England and II of Scotland and Mary II

Jacobean Nightcaps

Embroidered nightcaps and coifs are one of the most common items of costume to survive from the seventeenth century. During this period houses could be very cold and draughty, with the only sources of heat being wood-burning fires that did not always emit much heat beyond the immediate vicinity. Headwear was worn indoors as well as outdoors not only as a matter of propriety but also for the practical factor of warmth. In addition, many believed that wearing some form of head covering indoors would protect a person from ailments such as colds and headaches.

Traditionally, plain linen nightcaps, sometimes known as 'biggins', were worn in bed at night. Prince Hal in Shakespeare's *Henry IV, part 2*, remarks 'Yet not so sound and half so deeply sweet as he whose brow with homely biggen bound snores out the watch of night'.[1] By the end of the sixteenth and into the early seventeenth century embroidered nightcaps became popular. The name of these embellished caps is a misnomer, as these nightcaps were not worn in bed, but were a type of informal undress wear known as *déshabillé* (undress), a relaxed dress style. According to seventeenth-century etiquette ladies and gentleman wore *déshabillé* in private at home and dressed in such could only receive visitors who were close personal friends of an equal or lesser rank, or trades people. When entertaining guests of a higher social standing the host family were required to wear formal dress. According to this tradition embroidered nightcaps should only have been worn by gentlemen at home in the privacy of their parlour or later in the century in their cabinet, the precursor of a library or study. Nevertheless, in the first two decades of the seventeenth century it was noted that some gentlemen wore these embellished nightcaps in public in London and even at the Royal court. Orazio Busino, the chaplain to the new Venetian ambassador who was presented to James VI and I in 1617, wrote in *Anglipotrida*, 1618, that in the King's presence chamber '[o]ccasionally some of the chief lords and the favourite wear on their heads richly embroidered caps there under the pretence of having some imaginary indisposition'.[2]

1 *Henry IV, part 2*, Act 4, Scene 5, lines 26–8.
2 Cited in Arnold (2008), 12.

Opposite Detail of fig. 16

In keeping with their use as informal wear embroidered nightcaps are only depicted in a few portraits of this period. It was customary for sitters to choose clothing and accessories they would be painted in for their portrait, whether worn or shown to one side, as indicators of their status and rank in society. Lord Chancellors were painted wearing their chain of office and soldiers wearing or standing next to their armour. It was generally only academics and members of the clergy who were shown wearing nightcaps as a signifier of their profession. An unusual inclusion of a richly embroidered nightcap is seen in the portrait of *Phineas Pett (1570–1647)*, about 1612

Fig. 12: Anonymous, *Phineas Pett*, about 1612. Oil on panel, 119 × 100 cm. National Portrait Gallery, London

Phineas Pett was an ambitious man who was first presented to James VI and I in 1607. He became Master of the Corporation of Shipwrights in 1616. He worked for both James and Charles I, who appointed him Principal Officer of the Navy and Chief Commissioner at Chatham.

28 *Seventeenth-century Costume*

3 Perrin (1918), cited in Vincent (2003), 79.

Fig. 13: Nightcap, British, about 1600–20 (29.135)

The *rinceau* design is embroidered with silver-gilt scrolling coils worked in plaited braid stitch with smaller tendrils in chain stitch curling around flowers and fruit predominately sewn in detached buttonhole stitch.

(fig. 12). Pett was neither a scholar nor a clergyman, but a Master Shipwright at Chatham. His decision to be depicted wearing a nightcap reflects a pretentious aspect of his character, alluding to a level of scholarship he did not have. His awareness of the significance of dress as an outward sign of importance is apparent in his autobiography, in which he wrote that despite his limited income he was 'contented to taken any pains to get something to apparel myself, which by God's blessing I performed before Easter next after, and that in very good fashion, always endeavouring to keep company with men of good rank far better than myself'.[3]

The design on Pett's nightcap, in which curling stems enclose a variety of floral motifs, appears on an extant example (fig. 13). This nightcap is decorated with fruit and nuts, including acorns, grapes and strawberries as well as

flowers, such as borage, daffodils, honeysuckles, roses and pansies (fig. 14). These decorative patterns with scrolling tendrils date back to antiquity, when the curling leaves of the acanthus were incorporated into the capital of Corinthian columns. This style of design, sometimes known as *rinceau* (foliage), continued during the medieval and Renaissance periods on a variety of objects, from illuminated manuscripts to architectural features. Benvenuto Cellini (1500–71), in his autobiography written between 1558 and 1562, describes how the design developed in Italy:

> It is true that in Italy we have several different ways of designing foliage; the Lombards, for example, construct very beautiful patterns by copying the leaves of bryony and ivy in exquisite curves, which are extremely agreeable to the eye; the Tuscans and Romans make a better choice, because they can imitate the leaves of the acanthus, commonly called bear's-foot, with its stalks and flowers, curling in many divers wavy lines; and into these arabesques one may excellently well insert the figures of little birds and different animals, by

Fig. 14: Detail of the embroidery in fig. 13 – pansy

The pansy, commonly known as heart's-ease, was a popular embroidery motif appearing on jackets, nightcaps, coifs and gloves. It was a favourite flower of Queen Elizabeth I of England. When Elizabeth Talbot (1521–1608), Countess of Shrewsbury, sought advice in 1575 as to what would be a suitable New Year's gift for the monarch she was advised by Frances Radclyffe (1531–89), Countess of Sussex, to embroider a cloak with pansies as 'ye queen likes byst off that floware'.[4] Their name is said to have derived from the French term *pensée* meaning 'to think' and the flowers were often used to symbolize kind thoughts. The forsaken Ophelia in Shakespeare's *Hamlet* gives the flower to her brother Laertes, saying 'There's rosemary, that's for remembrance. Pray you, love, remember. And there is pansies, that's for thoughts.'[5]

which the good taste of the artist is displayed. Some hints for creatures of this sort can be observed in nature among the wild flowers, as for instance, in snapdragons and some few other plants, which may be combined and developed with the help of fanciful imaginings by clever draftsman.[6]

During the late sixteenth century and first two decades of the seventeenth century *rinceau* designs became particularly popular on embroidered garments in Britain, including women's jackets and coifs, as well as men's nightcaps.

The use of floral motifs within the design reflects the contemporary interest in natural history and in particular horticulture. Several printed sources were produced during this period including single-sheets and folios. Horticultural texts often combined botanical entries with artists' woodcuts of specimens and there were also increasing numbers of illustrated design books, such as John Overton and Peter Stent, *Flowers, Fruicts, Beastes, Birds and Flies*. Many designs for embroidery, including those for men's nightcaps, were copied from printed sources. Some early English pattern books produced during the sixteenth century were editions of continental publications; Adrian Poyntz, *New and singular patterns and works of linen*, 1591, was a copy of Federigo Vinciolo, *Les Singuliers et Nouveaux Pourtaicts et Ouvrages de Lingerie*, which had been published previously in Paris, Turin and Lyons. An influential British publication was Richard Shorleyker, *A Schole-House for the Needle*. Initially published in 1624, such was its popularity that it was in its twelfth edition by 1640. Several of the designs featured are similar to those found on embroidery dating from the 1540s onwards, suggesting that many had been in popular use for at least 80 years before he published them in his compendium. Thomas Trevelyon, in *Miscellany*, 1608, included alongside individual motifs several complete embroidery designs for men's nightcaps (fig. 15).[7]

There were several ways to transfer the outline of these designs from the page to the linen. One method was to prick small holes through the paper with the design and rub through powdered charcoal or pounce (cuttlefish bone) onto the ground fabric. Another method that was less damaging to the paper was to lay the printed design over the piece of cloth and prick holes along the pattern through both layers. The pinholes would have been visible on the finely woven

---

4 Folger, Cavendish-Talbot Letters, X.d.428 (128), Anthony Wingfield to Elizabeth Wingfield, 13 December 1575, cited in Arnold (1988), 94 and Howey (2007), 115.
5 *Hamlet*, Act 4, Scene 5, lines 194–5.
6 Pope-Hennessy (1995), 115–43, cited in Morrall and Watt (2008), 45.
7 MS V.b.232; formerly Folger MS 450517.

Fig. 15: Embroidery design from Thomas Trevelyon, *Miscellany*, 1608. Ink on paper. Folger Shakespeare Library, Washington DC

This large manuscript of over 290 double-sided folio pages is a compilation taken from a variety of sources such as almanacs and emblem books and covers a wide range of subjects.

linen and were then joined up with inked lines. Alternatively the cloth could be placed over the design and held against a light source, such as a window, allowing the motif or pattern to be traced. The drawing or copying of designs was often the work of draughtsmen. These were then either passed to professional embroiderers or the pre-drawn panels would be sold to amateurs to embroider at home.

The most common form of construction for nightcaps was for them to be made from a single piece of linen with the crown formed by cutting the top half of the cloth into a row of four deep conical points whilst the lower edge of the cloth was embroidered on the reverse side of the linen so that when folded back it would form the brim with the design facing out. As nightcaps did not need to be individually tailored they were not made to order but could be purchased ready-made. Frances Seymour (1578–1639), Countess of Hereford, instructed her steward in 1603 to visit the best embroiderer of nightcaps 'Mrs Price in the Strand' and buy a 'very fair one and not grossly wrought' of 'black silke and golde and silver'.[8] In 1629 an Oxford student, William Freke, bought a 'blackwork and gold cappe'

8 Cited in Vincent (2003), 48.
9 Bodleian Library, MSS. Eng. misc. c.201–3, c.338–9, cited in Gostelow (1976), 76.

for 17s 6d, the equivalent of three weeks' pay for a professional embroiderer.[9]

Nightcaps embroidered using black silk either alone, known as blackwork, or with metal threads, were as popular as the coloured silk versions, with contemporary depictions found in portraits, including Marcus Gheeraerts the Younger's portrait of *Richard Tomlins*, 1628, (Bodleian Library, Oxford). One particular nightcap, even though it only has two of its four panels remaining, is a good example of the technique (fig. 16). Whilst some areas of the black

Fig. 16: Nightcap, British, about 1600–20 (29.136)
A variety of stitches have been used to create this blackwork design, including chain, stem, split, double Pekinese, open Ceylon, woven wheels and various buttonhole stitches.

Fig. 17: Detail of the embroidery in fig. 16 – borage

Borage (*Borago officinalis*), also known as starflower due to its five pointed petals, was a popular plant as the flowers, which are commonly blue but can occasionally be pink, bloom for long periods of the year.

embroidery have deteriorated, enough survives to show the full design, which features a carnation at the apex of the conical panel that would have formed the peak of the crown. Below that, enclosed within coiling stems is a five-petal eglantine rose and honeysuckle and at the bottom is borage (fig. 17). As well as being decorated with floral motifs nightcaps could also be scented with flowers and herbs. William Turner in *A Newe Herball*, 1551, 'judge[s] that the flowers of the Lavender quilted in a cap and dayly worne are good for all diseases of the head that do come of a cold cause and they comfort the braine very well'.[10]

Another early seventeenth-century blackwork nightcap is embroidered with a regular pattern of berries or seeds, pods

10 Turner, (1551), cited in Synge (1982), 39.

Fig. 18: Nightcap, British, about 1600–20 (29.132)

The berries or seeds on this nightcap are embroidered in bullion knots, the long pods are in plaited braid stitch with silver gilt threads, whilst the leaves are in black silk thread with fillings worked in cross stitch.

and leaves (fig. 18). The design is duplicated on each of the four conical sections of the crown, with the floral motifs repeated along the brim. The finishing touches are lines of plaited braid stitch that were stitched over the seams on the crown once the nightcap was sewn up. The nightcap was previously in the collection of Major Currie, of Christleton, near Chester, but its earlier provenance is not known.

Nightcaps continued to be worn as items of *déshabillé* by gentlemen throughout the remainder of the seventeenth century and during the eighteenth century.

Jacobean Coifs

In many cultures it is customary for women to cover their head. In Christianity this can be dated to at least the middle of the first century AD when St Paul wrote his First Epistle to the Corinthians. His letter contains instructions as to the correct conduct during worship, including the command that women should cover their heads as to pray with bare heads is dishonourable.[1] This custom often extended beyond worship to wider life, especially for married women who covered their hair not only in public but often at home too. The coif – a kind of close-fitting cap – was worn informally at home by women in all levels of society during the sixteenth century and early-to-mid seventeenth centuries. For the majority of Elizabeth I's reign white linen coifs were favoured, either worn by themselves or under hoods and bonnets. However, in the 1590s to 1620s embroidered linen coifs became fashionable for aristocratic, gentry and wealthy middle-class women to wear at home. Some coifs were embroidered by the wearers or members of their household at home using a pre-drawn design. The Howard Accounts from the 1620s include a payment for 'drawing 2 coifs for my lady's and for the cloth 12d'.[2]

The majority of surviving examples appear to have been worked by professional embroiderers, who were often men. Considering how many must have been employed it is interesting to note how few references to professional embroiderers survive. One exception is a description by Lord Tales in George Chapman, *Sir Giles Goosecap*, 1606:

> He will worke you any flower to the life, as like it as if it grewe in the verie place, and being a delicate perfumer, hee will give it you his perfect and naturall savour ... He will make you flyes and worms of all sortes, most lively, and is now working on a whole bed embrodered with nothing but glowe wormes whose lightes has so perfectly domes, that you may goe to bed in the chamber, doe any thing in the Chamber, without a candle.[3]

A wonderful example of a professionally made coif is embroidered with a lively design in blue, red, yellow and

Opposite Detail of fig. 24

1 The Bible, 1 Corinthians 11: 5.
2 Cited in Brooks (2004), 72.
3 Act 2, Scene 1, cited in Arthur (1995), 24.

green silk threads (fig. 19). This coif is unfinished and consequently was never worn. As a result the colours are still as vibrant today as when they were first embroidered. The coif is decorated with the *rinceau* pattern with coiling stems enclosing flowers, such as carnations, pansies and honeysuckle. There are also acorns, strawberries and a large pomegranate bursting open with yellow and green seeds. The most striking feature of the design is the menagerie of both real and mythological animals. Amongst the former are some associated with the five senses; a dog representing smell, a monkey eating an apple for taste and a stag for hearing. Vices are symbolized by a boar for lust and a wyvern – a mythical creature with a dragon's head and serpent's body – for cruelty (fig. 20). The lion and leopard are often found in heraldry, where they represent the monarchy. There are also three snakes denoting wisdom, logic, and healing, of which the last dates back to Ancient Greece, when snakes were associated with Asclepius, the god of medicine. Another popular source for designs and motifs was Jacques le Moyne des Morgues's book *La Clef des champs, pour trouver plusiers Animaux, tant Bestes qu'Oyseaux, avec plusiers Fleurs et Fruit*, 1586. Published in London, it was

Fig. 19: Coif, British, about 1610–20 (29.22)

The various motifs on the coif are embroidered in buttonhole, detached buttonhole, and buttonhole eyelet stitches, as well as long-armed cross, individual Italian cross, stem, double-running and straight stitches and bullion knots. Red, blue, green and yellow silks have been used to create intermediate colours by twisting two different coloured threads together.

Fig. 20: Detail of embroidery in fig. 19 – wyvern

Wyverns are legendary creatures with the head and forelegs of a dragon and the body of a snake. They appear in British heraldry and were popular in the West Country and Wales, especially around the River Wye.

4 Carey (2009), 48.
5 Arnold (2008), 47.

dedicated to Madame Sydney as a source of inspiration 'for embroidery, tapestry and also for all kinds of needlework.'[4]

Several of the heads of the embroidered creatures on the coif are unfinished and in some instances reveal the original drawing underneath. The dress historian Janet Arnold (1932–98) suggested that the maker may have intended to work these at the end using metal threads.[5] The fact that the top and curving side edges are hemmed in green silk buttonhole stitch whilst the heads are still incomplete gives us a clear indication as to the order in which coifs were worked; first the silk work and then the metal work. Along the bottom the edge is left plain and would have been turned up after the completion of the embroidery to form the casing for a drawstring to be threaded through.

Jacobean Coifs

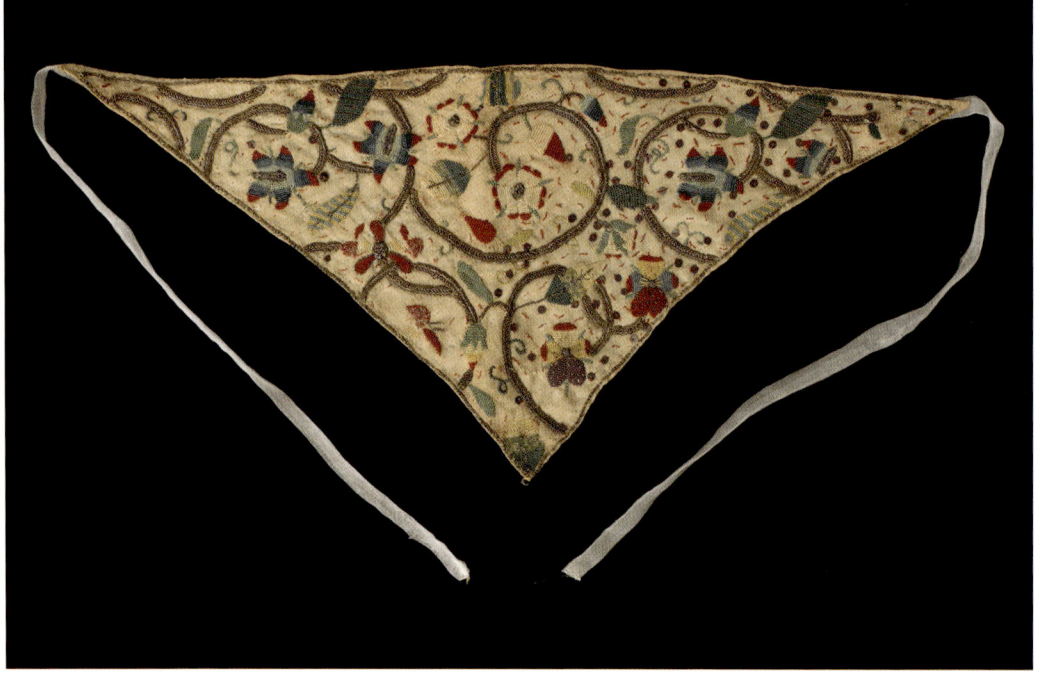

Opposite **Fig. 21: Coif and forehead cloth, British, about 1610–20 (29.134)**

Like many of the items of costume from this period decorated with the *rinceau* pattern the flowers and fruit are in coloured silk threads worked predominately in detached buttonhole stitch. The coiling stems and tendrils are embroidered in plaited braid stitch with silver-gilt threads known as passing. These threads have a silk core, white for silver and yellow for silver-gilt, around which narrow strips of the metal are wrapped.

An example of a woman's coif with a matching forehead cloth or cross-cloth is embroidered with a more typical *rinceau* design (fig. 21). Motifs include honeysuckles, pansies and roses as well as borage and strawberries. The last two were often depicted together as the horticultural practice of companion planting the two plants to make them grow better was well known by this period. The coif is decorated further with small metal discs, known as spangles, which would have twinkled whenever they caught the light. Matching sets of coifs and forehead cloths were common from at least the late sixteenth century. Queen Elizabeth I's New Year's gift rolls include two, 'a night coyf of cameryck cutwork and spangills, with a forehead cloth' in 1577–78 and 'a quoft and forehead cloth flourished with gold and silver' in 1588–89.[6] Meanwhile, the Warrants of Elizabeth's Wardrobe of Robes for 3 April 1588 include what may have been a complementary rather than matching coif and forehead cloth;

> one Coyfe of fine camerike wrought with blak silke edged with white silke lase
> one forehed cloth of camerike wrought with blak silke drawne worke edged with blak and white silke nedleworke lase.[7]

It is believed that forehead clothes were worn by women when they were ill or lying-in before and after childbirth, as mentioned in Fynes Moryson's *An Itinerary*, 1617, '[a]nd very many weare such crosse-clothes or forehead clothes as our Women use when they are sicke'.[8] It has been a subject of much debate among dress historians as to how the forehead cloth would have been worn or attached to the coif. Unfortunately, where forehead cloths survive they are rarely attached to their matching coif. Moreover there are no known depictions in portraits or sculpture of this type of embroidered coif with a forehead cloth to confirm how they would have been worn. The current consensus of opinion is that the triangular forehead clothes were put on first, with the long edge worn horizontally over the forehead, and the tapes from the corners either pinned to the hair towards the back of the head or tied into the nape of the neck. The point would lie over the top of the head and be held in place once the coif was put on over it (fig. 22).

---

6 Wingfield-Digby (1964), 73.
7 Arnold (2008), 46.
8 Morrison (1617), 227, cited in Cunnington (1955), 114.

When Sir William Burrell acquired the coif in 1936 from Frank Partridge & Sons it was sewn up with the forehead cloth attached over the coif (fig. 23). A photograph of it was published in the *Illustrated London News* a few months earlier with a caption that stated: 'An Elizabeth woman's cap discovered intact in an old country house, showing the manner in which these caps were, in fact, worn; with the point directed backwards.'[9] When the items were examined in the early 1980s it was discovered that the coloured silks on the coif under where the forehead cloth was attached were less faded than the surrounding areas, which suggests the coif and forehead cloth had been sew together for some period of time. However the coif in this form is upside-down. The speculation is that some previous owner, possibly

Fig. 22: Reconstruction of the coif with forehead cloth from fig.21

The coif and forehead cloth as they would have been worn together. The triangular forehead cloth would have had ties on its two acute points that passed around the head and fastened at the back. The coif was placed over to conceal the ties.

---

9 (1936) *Illustrated London News*, volume 189, no. 5085, 533.

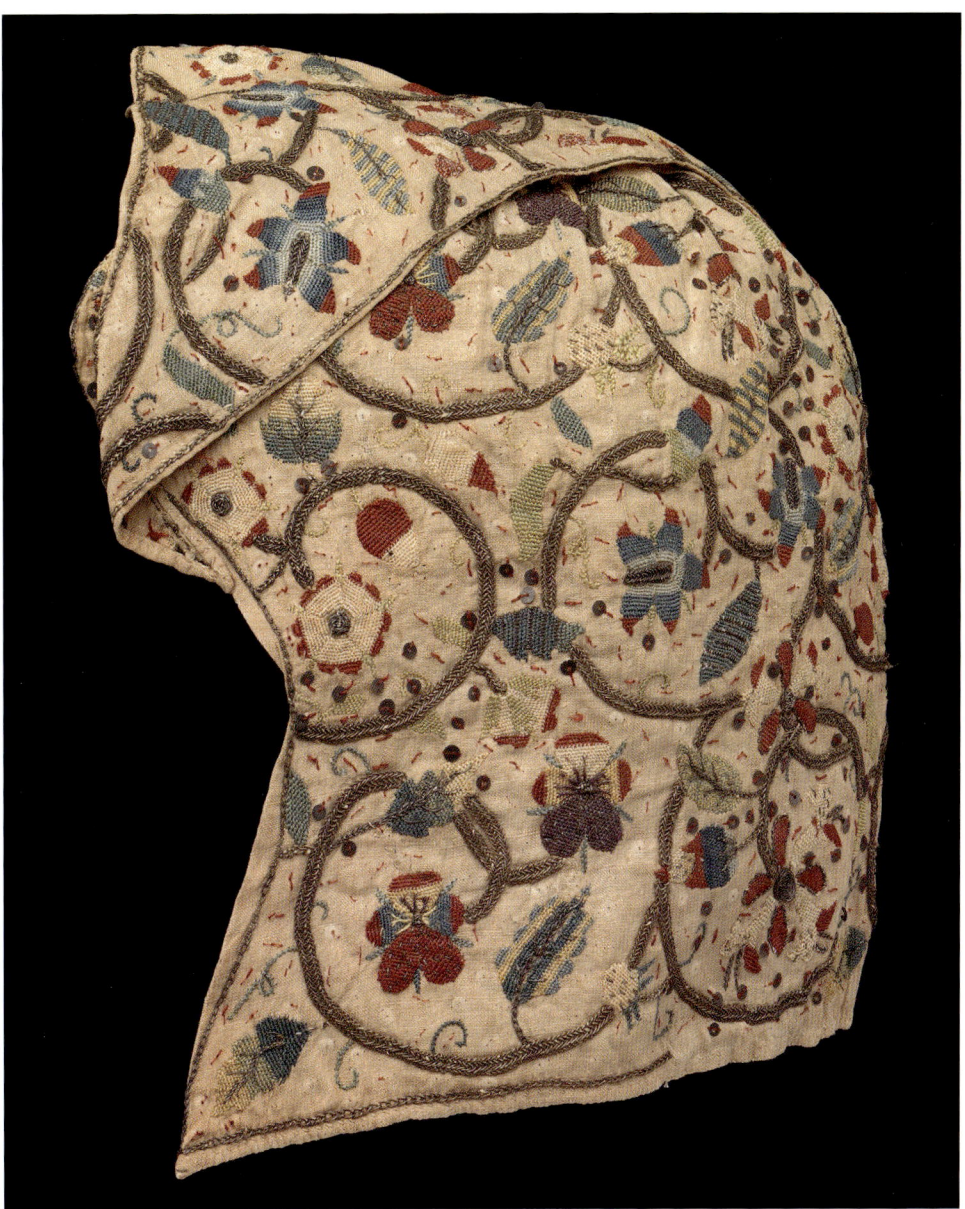

Fig. 23: Earlier construction of coif with forehead cloth from fig. 21

It is surprising that neither Frank Partridge (1875–1953) nor Sir William Burrell noticed that the pansies on the coif were upside down in this late eighteenth- or early nineteenth-century interpretation of how it would been made.

in the nineteenth century, mistook the creasing where a drawstring had tightened the bottom of the coif into the nape of the neck for what were fold lines along the top edge where it was gathered originally into the crown and decided to reconstruct the coif and forehead cloth, albeit incorrectly.

Some coifs suffered more extreme mishaps during the nineteenth century, when they were cut down by collectors

Fig. 24: Coif, British, about 1610–20 (29.17)

The *rinceau* design on this cut-down coif is not arranged as regularly as it first appears. Nor was it scaled to fit the height of the panel, as the fourth row only ever had its upper half worked.

10 Victoria and Albert Museum, London, T.75-1954.

of embroidery to form rectangular panels that could be framed more easily. This is probably what happened to a couple of small embroidered pieces including one that is decorated with a densely embroidered example of the *rinceau* pattern (fig. 24). Whilst the curved outer edges of the coif were cut off, the chain stitch lines top and bottom that edged the design along the central section can clearly be seen. The needlework is exquisitely worked, often using strands of silver-gilt or silver threads together with coloured silk threads to create the flowers, foliage and birds (fig. 25).

Another example of a coif that has been cut down is embroidered only in silver and silver-gilt threads (fig. 26). The sole use of expensive metal threads is found on a similarly ornate nightcap in the Victoria and Albert Museum, London.[10] The coiling stems of the *rinceau* design each end in a flower, including borage, carnations and honeysuckles, and fruit such as acorns, strawberries and peapods (fig. 27). The smaller scale of the design on this coif makes it easier to see the repeat of the pattern every four

Fig. 25: Detail of embroidery in fig. 24
The variety of stitches used on this coif includes Ceylon, chain, detached buttonhole, double buttonhole and up-and-down buttonhole, stem and woven wheel stitches. It is further decorated with metal spangles sewn on with red silk thread.

Below Fig. 26: Coif, British, about 1610–20 (29.21)
A fine example of a coif worked entirely in silver and silver-gilt threads using a wide range of stitches such as basketwork, buttonhole, chain, Ceylon, open Ceylon, plaited braid and woven wheel stitch.

Jacobean Coifs

Fig. 27: Detail of embroidery in fig. 26 – peapod

Peapods, or peascods, with their clearly visible seeds were associated with courtship and fertility. The inclusion of such symbols is suggestive of the more intimate nature of the parlour and bed chamber, where coifs would have been worn in private.

columns and three rows. At the top a line of chain stitch marks the vertical edge of the design. The plain border along the bottom edged with looped threads is where the drawstring could have been threaded.

An historic reuse for coifs after they were no longer fashionable was for them to be made into other items. During conservation work in 1987 a small cushion was discovered to have been made using a coif for its top cover. Fortuitously the curved edges were not cut off in this instance, but merely folded in and seamed to the velvet back. When the cushion was unpicked the full shape of the coif was revealed (fig. 28).

Fig. 28: Coif, British, about 1610–20 (29.294.a)
This coif, acquired by Sir William Burrell as a small cushion, still shows signs of this later use where the linen ground has discoloured and the silver and silver-gilt threads are tarnished from exposure to atmospheric pollutants.

Below Fig. 29: Coif, British, about 1610–15 (29.130)
The main design of this coif is worked in chain-stitched silver thread with small details worked in twisted and laid or couched threads.

Fig. 30: Detail of embroidery in fig. 29
Flower motifs have been created by cutting into the linen, turning back the edges and creating decorative fillings in detached buttonhole stitch and needle-weaving.

A more unusual combination of techniques to create the *rinceau* design is found on a coif that uses simpler embroidery stitches with needle-weaving centres to the various motifs, including birds, gillyflowers, daffodils, eglantine roses and leaves (fig. 29). The application of these techniques is close to that found on a slightly earlier coif dated about 1575–1600 in the Untermeyer Collection at the Metropolitan Museum of Art, New York, which has softer curls and more detailed fillings.[11] The embroidery is worked in silver threads which would have been much lighter in appearance when originally made so that the decoration would have resembled whitework embroidery. The silver thread and additional silver spangles would have twinkled as they caught the flickering light of candles or the fire in the evening (fig. 30). Francis Bacon, in 'Of Masques and Triumphs', *Essays*, 1597, suggests that '[t]he Colours, that shew best by Candlelight are; White Carnation, and a Kinde of Sea-Water-Greene; and Oes, or Spangs, as they are of no great Cost, so they are of most Glory. … As for Rich Embroidery, it is lost, and not Discerned'.[12] Today the silver threads and spangles are tarnished, their surfaces oxidized and dark despite careful cleaning, giving an appearance that is closer to blackwork.

11 Irwin Untermeyer collection, Metropolitan Museum of Art 64.101.1240, illustrated in Morrall and Watt (2008), 172.

12 Bacon, (1625), cited in Vincent (2003), 38.

Blackwork

Linen embroidered with a monochromatic design in black silk thread is known as blackwork. It is believed to have originated in the Middle East and was introduced to Europe through the Moors of Spain in the late medieval period. It was first used as a method of decorating articles of dress in the second half of the fifteenth century. Catherine of Aragon (1485–1536) is said to have brought the style from Spain to England when she married Arthur Tudor (1486–1502), Prince of Wales, son of Henry VII (1457–1509), in 1501. Initially the designs were geometric, but during the century the style softened and variations of the scrolling *rinceau* pattern grew in popularity, reaching their peak during the 1590s to 1620s. Marcus Gheeraerts the Younger's portrait of *Mary Throckmorton, Lady Scudamore*, 1615 (fig. 31) shows a waistcoat embroidered with blackwork. As befits the status of the wearer, the embroidery on this outfit was worked by professionals. However, many patterns embroidered on the collars and cuffs of women's chemises and men's shirts were worked by amateurs. Linen garments of this kind were made in most instances by women for their families, or by female servants in larger, wealthier households. Whilst the plain sewing of the seams would probably have been undertaken in private, the more decorative blackwork borders may have been deemed suitable to be done in front of visitors as a demonstration of the lady's skill.

In contrast to the intricate blackwork depicted in the portrait, the border on a linen handkerchief was stitched by an amateur embroiderer, possibly the original owner (fig. 32). The design of repeated stylized, almost geometric, floral motifs sewn, predominately in black silk thread using cross stitch, appears to have been worked by eye rather than counted as no two are the same. Even the layout is uneven with a different number of flowers along each edge ranging from seven to nine-and-a-half. The narrow outer border has a chevron pattern worked in cross stitch with silver-gilt thread in running stitch. At the top right corner are the owners initials 'MQ'. The flowers

Opposite Detail of fig. 34

Fig. 31: Marcus Gheeraerts the Younger, *Mary Throckmorton, Lady Scudamore*, 1615. Oil on canvas, 114.3 × 82.6 cm. National Portrait Gallery, London

The waistcoat is embroidered with curling stems with ermine tails in black silk thread with small silver-gilt spangles.

Fig. 32: Handkerchief, British, about 1600–25 (29.148)

The carnation border is embroidered in black silk thread using cross stitch with details in silver-gilt thread worked in chain, plaited braid, satin and woven wheel stitch.

Fig. 33: Detail of embroidery in fig. 32 – carnation

Carnations (*Dianthus caryophyllus*) are thought to have originated from around the Mediterranean but have been cultivated since ancient times. Their scientific name *Dianthus* derives from the Greek for 'heavenly flower'. They are associated with the Virgin Mary's grief and have become symbolic of a mother's love. The flowers are also known as 'gilly flowers', a design for which was included in Jacques le Moyne *La Clef des Champs*, 1586.[1] The early seventeenth-century English gardener William Lawson, in *The Country Housewife's Garden*, 1631, states that they are 'of all the flowers (save the damask rose) the most pleasant in sight and smell'.[2]

---

1. Gostelow (1976), 74.
2. Lawson (1631), 91, cited in Gostelow (1976), 74.

Fig. 34: Coif, British, about 1610–20 (29.131)

The rows of thin coiling stems and five-petal flowers are embroidered in black silk thread using stem and outline stitch. The plain rows have zig-zag borders worked in back or double-running stitch with silver and silver-gilt spangles.

themselves are probably carnations, which were a popular motif during this period (fig. 33).

Many items of late sixteenth-century and early seventeenth-century blackwork have areas where the silk threads have degraded, resulting in the patterns and motifs being slowly lost and leaving only the tiny holes where the thread had passed through the ground cloth as evidence of the embroidered design. One example is a coif embroidered with a bold diagonal design (fig. 34). Where the black silk thread is lost not only are the thread holes visible, but also the original inked design.

Blackwork 53

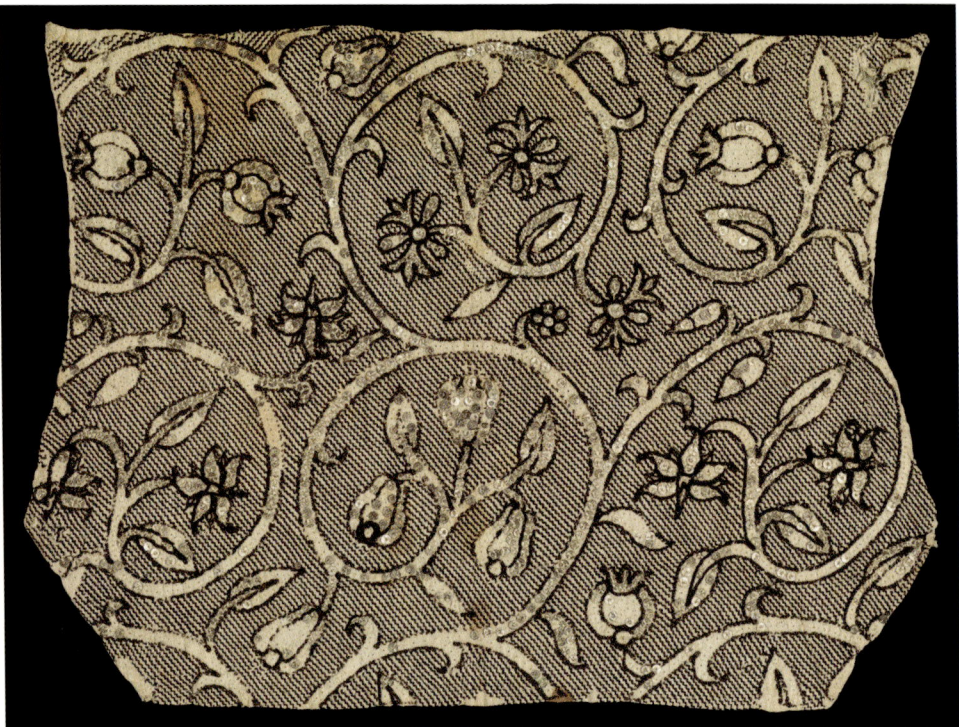

Fig. 35: Panel of blackwork, British, about 1600–20 (29.137)

The outline design is created with couched twisted black silk thread. The background is shaded with diagonal rows of single faggot stitch that is for the main part stitched from top left to bottom right.

Creating a good quality black dye that does not appear dark brown, blue or grey, has traditionally been a challenge. One of the oldest sources in Britain for producing black was the plant woad (*Isatis tinctoria*). This is a non-native plant that has been cultivated widely in Europe since the Iron Age. Woad produces a blue dye that if made in a strong enough concentration and mixed with further vegetable matter could be used to make black. Another popular black dye was iron tannate. This was created with tannic acid from alder or oak bark mixed with gall nut. It required an iron mordant, or fixative, to fix the dye to the yarn or cloth. During the sixteenth and seventeenth centuries woad began to be replaced by indigo (*Indigofera tinctoria*) that also required an iron mordant. The chemical composition of these dyes also proved to be problematic, causing the silk threads to weaken and eventually disappear. Today it is known that it is the iron in these dyes that causes this degradation as a result of the metal oxidizing in contact with air; however, in the early modern period it was believed to be the indigo. As early as 1532 the English parliament placed embargos on the importation of indigo and there was a

3 Hurry (1930).
4 *A Midsummer Night's Dream*, Act 4, Scene 1, lines 39 and 41.

long-held belief that it was poisonous. One German state banned indigo in 1557, referring to it as 'the newly-invented, deceitful, eating and corrosive dye called the devil's dye.'³

A small panel of blackwork is unusual for having a reverse effect to the design with the *rinceau* pattern void except for small spangles whilst the background is embroidered with diagonal lines worked in single faggot stitch (fig. 35). The motifs here include borage, pomegranates, pears and honeysuckle (fig. 36). This piece was catalogued until recently as a coif, due to its shape, but it is too narrow to have been made as a coif originally. It is more likely that the piece was cut down from a larger item of costume, which has then had the two bottom corners turned in at a later date. The horizontal measurements and diameter of curves at the side, without seam allowance, closely follow the pattern of the upper part of the central back panel on the woman's embroidered waistcoat discussed in the next chapter. This may suggest one possibility for the panel's original use.

Fig. 36: Detail of embroidery in fig. 35 – honeysuckle

Honeysuckle (*Lonicera*) is a species of vine that needs to grow on a support and because of that particular characteristic is often used to symbolize affection and faithfulness. An early example of this is Marie de Breton, *Chevrefoil* (Honeysuckle), late twelfth century, which tells the story of the doomed love affair between Tristan and Iseult. Tristan is described as a hazel and Iseult the honeysuckle that, according to tradition, will entwine itself in such a manner about the tree that neither it nor the hazel can survive without the other. This literary motif is found later in William Shakespeare's play, *A Midsummer Night's Dream*, about 1594–6, in which the enamoured fairy queen Titania tells the Athenian weaver Bottom 'I will wind thee in my arms … so doth the woodbine the sweet honeysuckle gently entwist'.⁴

Embroidered Waistcoats

Waistcoats were commonly worn by men and women as undergarments for support and warmth during the sixteenth and seventeenth-century. The most basic were made in linen, but some were interlined and quilted and the wealthy had waistcoats in silk, with the finest decorated with embroidery. Queen Elizabeth had many fine examples that are listed in the warrants for the Wardrobe of Robes, including an entry in 1565 for David Smith who was paid:

> for enbrauderinge of a wastcote of white taphata sarceonet with a worke allover of black silke lyke a scallop Shell wrought upon fine lynen clothe for workemanship therof xlvjs. Item for viij oz of granado silke to worke the same at iijs thoz xxiiijs. Item for bombast spent upon the same wastcote ijs vjd.[1]

The inventory of Denmark House taken on 19 April 1619 after the death of Anne of Denmark includes 'fowrteene wastcotes of lynnon cloth two of them embrodered and the rest of them of needle-worcke'.[2]

During the sixteenth century waistcoats were viewed as undergarments and it was not deemed proper for the garment to be visible when worn in public. However, in the early 1600s there was a period when highly embroidered waistcoats were worn as outer garments by aristocratic and upper class ladies in public. Unlike the very lavish formal court dresses of the period, several of these embroidered waistcoats survive in museum collections, including one dating from about 1615–18 (fig. 37). These waistcoats were made by professional workshops. The ground fabric, of un-dyed, closely woven plain or tabby weave linen was first inked with the pattern pieces and design for the embroidery. The linen, held taut on frames, was then embroidered in three stages: the coloured silks, the metal threads and finally the metal spangles (fig. 38). The motifs on the waistcoat include caterpillars and butterflies (fig. 39) as well as flowers, such as borage and roses (fig. 40). Whilst several waistcoats of this type survive in museum collections, there are only two known at present to have been copied from the same design, the waistcoat in the

1 PRO, LC5/33, f.37, warrant dated 16 April 1565, cited in Arnold (1988), 145.

2 Payne (2001), 40.

Opposite Detail of fig. 37

Fig. 37: Waistcoat, British, about 1615–18 (29.127)

The motifs, which include borage and eglantine roses, foliage, caterpillars and butterflies, are embroidered in silk threads predominantly worked in detached buttonhole stitch.

Opposite top **Fig. 38: Embroidered panel, British, about 1610–20 (29.26)**

This small embroidered panel, worked with a similar *rinceau* design in coloured silks and silver-gilt thread, may have been cut down from an upper back panel of a waistcoat. The curve on the left edge is of a similar radius to where the sleeve would have been attached.

Opposite bottom **Fig. 39: Detail of embroidered butterfly on waistcoat**

The wings on the butterfly are embroidered in green, pink and blue silk thread shaded by using two colours together. They are edged using silver thread with chain stitch and decorated with woven wheel spots.

58   *Seventeenth-century Costume*

Fig. 40: Detail of embroidered roses on waistcoat from fig. 37

The sweet briar or eglantine rose (*Rosa rubiginosa*) is shown open with five petals. The rose is a common symbol in Christianity, associated not only with Jesus Christ but also with the Virgin Mary. In medieval romances the rose symbolized love, especially courtly love, as depicted in Guillaume de Lorris, *Le Roman de la Rose*, written during the thirteenth century. The flower became a particularly important symbol during the fifteenth and sixteenth centuries in England, when it was used to signify the two conflicting Plantagenet dynasties during the Wars of the Roses. The red rose was chosen as the symbol of the ruling House of Lancaster and the white rose by their rivals, the House of York. When Henry Tudor of Lancaster won the Battle of Bosworth in 1485 to become Henry VII he married Elizabeth of York (1466–1503) and famously combined the two roses to form the heraldic red and white Tudor rose that was used throughout the sixteenth century. When James VI inherited the throne in 1603 the Tudor rose ceased to be used, but the eglantine rose continued to be a popular floral motif.

Burrell Collection and one on loan from a private collection to the Fashion Museum, Bath (fig. 41). The needlework pattern has been carefully worked out to provide symmetry to both the front and back of the waistcoat. Further decoration was added with small metal spangles sewn scattered on the plain areas of linen. Most of these are now lost, but upon closer inspection it is possible to see the tiny holes that once held the silk thread that attached them. With time the metal has oxidized and corroded the filaments of the thread, eventually causing them to break and the spangle to be lost.

After the embroidery was completed the panels were cut out and stitched to form the waistcoat with three main pieces for the bodice; centre back and two front panels that extend around the sides of the body. The garment is fitted by the tailoring at waist and additional v-shaped gored panels inserted over the hips at the front and sides, and one in the middle of the back. The collar was embroidered and cut separately, as were the epaulettes and full-length sleeves. The cuffs were made in one piece with the sleeves and embroidered on the reverse side, allowing the pattern to show once the cuffs were folded back. This had the advantage that when lining the sleeves and cuffs there were only three pieces of fabric, rather than four, with fewer hem

Fig. 41: Embroidered waistcoat, British, about 1610–20. Linen embroidered in silk, silver and silver-gilt thread and spangles, centre-back 48 cm. Fashion Museum, Bath

The design of the flowers and coiling stems is almost identical on both the Burrell and Bath waistcoats. In addition, the main coils of the *rinceau* design worked in plaited braid stitch in silver-gilt threads have an unusual border of small red motifs either side.

Embroidered Waistcoats 61

or seam allowances. In the majority of instances the plaited braid stitched coils lined up when two panels were sewn together to form the waistcoat, but there are a couple of places where the v-shaped gored panels have been inserted into the back of the waistcoat so that the designs are slightly out of alignment. Finally, most of the seams, but not all, were hidden with a row of plaited braid stitch to match the coiling stems.

Unlike some surviving waistcoats that are fastened with silk bows at the front this example is fastened with 21 hooks and eyes. The three at the waist made of a thick dark-grey metal wire, possibly steel, may be original.[3] The remainder are later replacements made from brass, although still historic, added during the late seventeenth or eighteenth century. Brass and steel hooks and eyes survive on several items of clothing from the sixteenth and early seventeenth century. Queen Elizabeth I's tailors are recorded as ordering them by the pound.[4] An early example of the use of hooks and eyes to fasten clothing is found in Jean Fouquet's painting *The Ferrara Court Jester, Gonella*, about 1442, (Kunsthistorisches Museum, Vienna).[5] The sitter is depicted wearing a patchwork doublet with the collar left unfastened and open to reveal two pairs of hooks and eyes of the same design as those available today.

Like many other similar extant embroidered waistcoats, this waistcoat has no provenance and it is not known who it belonged to originally. A rare exception is the embroidered waistcoat worn by Margaret Layton (fig. 42). Margaret Layton (died 1641) was the daughter of Sir Hugh Browne, a rich merchant in the City of London. She married Frances Layton (1573–1661), who later became one of the Yeoman of the Jewel House. What makes this a specifically interesting example is that it was worn by an aspirational middle-class woman. There are several other portraits from about 1610–20 in which embroidered waistcoats are depicted, such as in William Larkin, *Lady Dorothy Cary* (died 1628), about 1615 (fig. 43), but the wearers are all aristocratic ladies of the Jacobean court. A small number of these portraits show the waistcoats cut with a very low oval décolletage, exposing most of the fashionably low, flat breasts. These often show the women wearing their hair down and a silk sash over one shoulder, which suggests that these outfits may have been worn for court masques, a

3 Arnold (1985), 51, 120–1.
4 Arnold (1988), 181.
5 Tarrant (1996), 20.

Fig. 42: Attributed to Marcus Gheeraerts the Younger, *Margaret Layton*, about 1620 with embroidered waistcoat worn by Margaret Layton, British, about 1610–15, with possible alterations 1620–25. Oil on oak panel, 81.5 × 62.5 cm. Victoria and Albert Museum, London

The portrait of Margaret Layton depicts the sitter at a slightly later date from when her waistcoat was made. The fashions had altered slightly by then and her red silk petticoat and diaphanous apron are shown worn over the basque of the waistcoat rather than under it. Linen with silk and silver-gilt thread, spangles, centre-back 68 cm.

favoured pastime of Anne of Denmark. However, the majority of waistcoats in the portraits, like many surviving examples, have a high round neckline and were worn with an intricate lace band supported on a wired rebato frame and matching cuffs.

Lace was a luxury item during the late sixteenth and seventeenth centuries, becoming an essential part of both fashionable men's and women's wardrobes. Its use as a form of conspicuous consumption is evidenced by the detailed attention paid to replicating the intricate designs in contemporary portraits. In many instances the lace depicted is *reticella*, the earliest form of needle lace. It developed during the sixteenth century from embroidered cutwork where a grid is created in a piece of linen, by cutting or drawing out threads in the cloth, and then embroidered using varieties of detached buttonhole stitch. As cutwork evolved the holes became larger so that often

Embroidered Waistcoats 63

Fig. 44: *Reticella* with *dentate punto in aria* edging, Venetian, late 16th–early 17th century (1888.19.k)

It is just possible to see the thin lines of the grid from the original linen cloth on this example of lace. The spaces have been filled with a stylized design incorporating eagles with eyes made from black beads.

only a skeletal grid was left, which was then stitched to form the *reticella* lace. Soon lace-makers realized that it was possible to create the grid using only threads, rather than cutting and drawing out threads from a cloth, and started making *punto in aria* ('holes in the air'). Often the two techniques were combined with *punto in aria* edgings made separately and then attached to a length of *reticella* lace, as seen on an example in Glasgow's collection (fig. 44). The points along the edge on this piece suggest that it may have been used to make a band or cuff.

Lady Dorothy Cary's outfit is completed with a full-length black silk gown decorated with a rich silk and metal thread border worn over a richly worked silk satin petticoat. Unlike embroidered linen waistcoats, surviving examples of gowns and skirts are extremely rare.

Opposite Fig. 43: William Larkin, *Lady Dorothy Cary*, about 1615. Oil on canvas, 205.9 × 122.1 cm. English Heritage, Kenwood House, Suffolk Collection, London

This portrait depicts a more informal style of dressing with the waistcoat worn with an equally lavish embroidered petticoat; the softer line of the latter created by being worn over a padded bum roll rather than the formal French or wheel farthingale.

Embroidered Petticoat

The vibrant portraits of aristocratic ladies at the court of James VI and I and Queen Anne of Denmark often show the women wearing embroidered or painted silk skirts with their embroidered linen waistcoats. These skirts were typically known during the early seventeenth century as petticoats, derived from the French phrase *petit cote* or little coat.

An incredibly rare surviving example of a petticoat is made in carnation red silk satin (fig. 45). The central section is relatively plain with only small, regularly spaced, motifs in the shape of ermine tails, each with three silver spangles stitched on with French knots and the fourth held in place with long stitches to create the tails. The pattern is similar to that embroidered on cuffs in the portrait attributed to Daniel Mytens, *Elizabeth Howard (1586–1658), Countess of Banbury*, about 1615–20 (figs. 46 and 47).[1] Around the edge of the petticoat is a deep border with a large repeat on each panel running along the lower edge of the skirt and up both short sides (fig. 48). The elegant *rinceau*-style pattern encloses various flowers together with birds, butterflies and insects and is drawn in with regular peaks along its inside edge, with a thistle prominently displayed at each apex (fig. 49).

The prominent placing of thistles in the design gave rise to an apocryphal story that the skirt was embroidered by Mary, Queen of Scots (1542–87). Margaret Swain, in *The Needlework of Mary, Queen of Scots*, 1973, contains an account of a red skirt embroidered by Mary to give to her cousin, Elizabeth I, in 1574 during her long period of captivity in England.[2] Earlier that year Mary had written to the French ambassador in London requesting the purchase of sufficient red silk to make a skirt:

> I must give you the trouble of acting for me in smaller matters, viz. to send me as soon as you can eight ells of crimson satin of the colour of the sample silk which I send you, the best that can be found in London, but I should like to have it in fifteen days, and one pound of the thinner and double silver thread….

1 Unpublished correspondence from Janet Arnold, 1996, in Glasgow Museums' archives.
2 Swain (1973), 82–83.

Opposite Detail of fig. 45

Fig. 45: Petticoat, British, about 1610–20 (29.314)

The petticoat is made from six widths of silk satin using the full breadth of the fabric with the seams sewn along the selvedges. The four inner widths are formed from two square panels each, rather than one long rectangular panel. Traditionally in Europe the best red dye was made from dried shield insects. The main variety was kermes (*Kermes vermilio* Planchon), a species that was native to Arles and the surrounding area in Provence and the Languedoc, and later cultivated along the Mediterranean coast. Smaller amounts of cochineal were available, either originating from the areas around Mount Ararat in Armenia (*Porphyrophora hameli* Brandt) and imported to Venice, Genoa and Marseille, or from Poland (*Porphyrophora polonicai* L), sometimes known as Saint John's blood.[3] Cochineal was preferred to kermes because it was thought to have ten times the dyeing strength and it soon became a luxury good. The growing popularity of crimson red as a symbol of wealth and importance led to Pope Paul II's (1417–71) decree in 1467 that cardinals' robes would be dyed red using cochineal instead of Tyrian purple. After the Spanish conquest of Mexico under Hernán Cortés (1485–1547) in the 1520s the major source of cochineal became Central America. Vast new supplies of cochineal (*Dactylopius coccus* Costa found on the prickly pear cactus) were imported from New Spain to Spain from whence it was sold in insect or powdered form. Spain held the monopoly on this trade for the majority of the century. Merchants in Antwerp, which was then part of the Spanish Netherlands, sold cochineal on to the textile industry in northern Europe from the 1530s.

---

3 Buss (2009), 167.
4 Swain (1973), 83.
5 Unpublished correspondence from Janet Arnold and Santina Levey, 1996, in Glasgow Museums' archives.

The skirt was finished with a crimson satin lining in May and Mary asked the French ambassador to present it to Elizabeth I on her behalf 'as evidence of the honour I bear her'. Later that month the French ambassador wrote of its presentation in his letter to Charles IX of France (1550–74):

> 'The Queen of Scots, your sister-in-law, is very well, and yesterday I presented on her behalf a skirt of crimson satin, worked in silver, very fine and all worked by her own hand, to the Queen of England, to whom the present was very agreeable, for she found it very nice and has prized it much; and she seemed to me that I found her much softened towards her'.

Margaret Swain suggests that the surviving red petticoat fits this description, but that '[t]he design is elegant and stylish, and if worked by Mary would seem to be a little in advance of contemporary English fashion'.[4]

When the petticoat was examined by dress and textile historians Janet Arnold and Santina Levey when it was purchased by the Burrell Trustees in 1996 it was re-dated to 1610–20.[5] The arabesque floral and foliage ornamentation is similar in style to embroidery designs published in Johann Sibmacher's books, *Schon neues Modelbuch*, 1597, and *Fysirvngen zum Vereichnen fur did Goldtschmidt*, 1601. The embroidery would have been by professional embroiderers, often at great expense; Lady Anne Clifford (1590–1676) paid £80 in 1617 for the

Fig. 46: Attributed to Daniel Mytens, *Elizabeth Howard (1586–1658), Countess of Banbury*, about 1615–20. Oil on canvas, 213.4 × 142.6 cm. English Heritage, Kenwood House, Suffolk Collection, London

Elizabeth Howard's black gown is complemented by a linen waistcoat embroidered in blackwork. The skirt of her gown is open at the front to reveal a petticoat or single panel, known as a forepart, underneath embroidered to match the waistcoat.

Embroidered Petticoat

Fig. 47: Detail of cuff in fig. 46

Below **Fig. 48:** Detail of embroidered border in fig. 45

Flat stitches such as satin and long-and-short stitch are used for the flowers, including daffodils, honeysuckle, lilies, pinks and roses, with several further decorated with overstitching for details. Acorn shells are edged with French knots and hearts are slightly padded and have a lattice of metal threads couched over. The coiling stems are worked in silver threads, known as passing, with metal plate spiral wrapped around a dark blue silk core.

embroidery alone worked in silk threads and seed pearls on a white satin gown for Anne of Denmark.[6] However, in contrast with the embroidered waistcoat discussed in the previous chapter, the type of stitches used for the flowers together with the use of couched metal thread instead of plaited braid stitch for the coils would have made this petticoat quicker to embroider than a waistcoat.

The petticoat was passed down by descent for over 350 years as an heirloom until it was purchased by the Burrell Trustees in 1996. According to family tradition the skirt had been given as a gift to William Dering, a page at the court of Charles I. It passed down the family to John Thurlow Dering Esq. of Crowhall (died 1837), was inherited by his daughter Anne, who married William Lee Warner, and had then descended via their daughter to the Bulwer family. It was, and still is, a custom for members of the Royal Household to receive personal gifts known as 'prerequisites' or perks. One common form of gift is clothes no longer required by the original wearer, so it is plausible that the petticoat was a gift from Charles I to one of his loyal retainers. Recent research on the provenance of the petticoat failed to find any William Dering. However, John Thurlow Dering's great-uncle, the Reverend Edward Dering (died 1719), married Catherine Levett, the daughter of William Levett. Levett was appointed to the role of Page of the Backstairs to Charles I and later promoted to Groom of the Chamber, becoming a known favourite of the king. Specifically, William was requested by Charles to attend him during his captivity at Carisbrooke Castle on the Isle of Wight and later he was one of the attendants at Charles I's execution at Whitehall, London, on 30 January 1649, bearing his body afterwards to be buried at St George's Chapel, Windsor Castle. During his time serving the monarch, William received several prerequisites as a reward for his loyal service. It is known that items relating to Charles I were later in the possession of William's close relatives, including his brother Reverend Richard Levett, his son Henry (1668–1725), and his nephew Sir Richard Levett (died 1711), Lord Mayor of London, who owned portraits by Sir Anthony Van Dyck (1599–1641) of Charles I and Queen Henrietta Maria. It is not improbable that Catherine, as his only surviving daughter, would have been given or inherited the embroidered petticoat. When Catherine and

---

6 Clifford (ed) (1992), 64, cited in Riberio (2005).

Fig. 49: Detail of embroidered thistle in fig. 45

Thistles are associated with sorrow in Christianity and used to represent the suffering of Jesus Christ. However, in the Celtic tradition they are associated with noble birth and character and are one of the national symbols of Scotland. The association dates back to the reign of Alexander III (1241–86) when the presence of an invading Norwegian army under the leadership of Haakon IV (1204–63) was given away when they stood barefoot on thistles.

her husband died without issue their estate and possessions passed into the Dering family. If the petticoat was given as a prerequisite by Charles I it is possible that it may have been made originally for his mother, Anne of Denmark.

Anne of Denmark had an extravagant taste in dress; by 1605 she had run up debts of over £40,000 on clothes.[7] When James VI of Scotland succeeded to the English throne in 1603, his wife inherited the majority of the former monarch's personal possessions. Scaramell, the Venetian Secretary, wrote that;

> In the late Queen's wardrobe [Anne of Denmark] found six thousand dresses, and though she declared that she would never wear cast clothes, still it was found that art could not devise anything more costly and gorgeous, and so the Court dressmakers are at work altering these old robes, for nothing new could surpass them.[8]

Anne's personal taste was similar to Elizabeth I, favouring expensive, often jewel-decorated gowns with stiffly boned bodices and skirts, known as petticoats, worn supported over cartwheel-shaped French farthingales. Many garments were

---

7 Clifford (ed) (1992), 64, cited in Riberio (2005).
8 Ibid.

remade for Anne, with several used to create masque costumes as recounted by Arbella Stuart (1575–1615) in a letter to Gilbert Talbot, Earl of Shrewsbury (1552–1616), on 18 December 1603, '[t]he Queene intendeth to make a mask this Christmas, to which end my Lady of Suffolk and my Lady of Walsingham have warrants to take of the late queen's best apparel out of the tower at their discretion'.[9] Other items were made new to order, both professionally or by her household. After her death in 1619 James VI and I ordered a series of inventories to be taken, including one of 'Remnantes of Stuffes of sundry kindes, olde Robes and Garmentes of former Queenes of this Realme with divers other thinges belonging unto our sade late Deere Consort'. Upon completion of the inventories James instructed the commissioners on 2 July 1619 that any:

> Apparell, Robbes and other furniture of our late Deere Consort, as were by her used and worne in her Lyfe tyme, and are not nowe meete to be by Us kepte and preserved, We are pleased, and by these Present doe require and geve Power and Authoritie unto you our said Commissioners, or anie three or more of you as aforesaid, amongst suche Ladies and others as served or attended uppon our said late Consort, in such a matter as you in your Wisdomes shall thinke meete.[10]

The inventory for Denmark House includes an entry for '[t]he skirtes of a gowne of white satten unmade upp embroidered wth gold and silke of divers Coulors in thither great Cipres Cheste'.[11] At present it has not been possible to trace all the inventories to find out if one contains a listing for a petticoat that matches the surviving one.

Another area of enquiry is how the petticoat might have been worn. The top edge of the petticoat has been altered and it is not possible to say for certain whether it was originally worn over a French farthingale or a padded bum roll. The French farthingale, also known as a great or wheel farthingale, was a petticoat with large circular hoops made of wicker or whalebone that produced a cylindrical silhouette. It was introduced in the 1570s and reached the height of popularity in the English and French courts in 1590s, and was retained by Anne of Denmark. The skirts that went over these large frames had additional material at the top to allow them to be folded and pinned into a horizontally pleated flounce around the waist each day. However, in the early

9 Steen (1994), 197, letter 36.
10 Payne (2001), 25.
11 Payne (2001), 41.

Fig. 50: Anonymous, *Elizabeth Home (about 1599–1633), Countess of Suffolk*, about 1615–17. Oil on canvas, 207 × 148 cm. English Heritage, Kenwood House, Suffolk Collection, London

Elizabeth Home's embroidered carnation red silk petticoat is still constructed with the loosely pleated fold around the waist, but is probably supported by a bum roll rather than a French farthingale.

decades of the seventeenth century a new softer line was brought back to court fashions by the adoption of the bum roll, an undergarment originally worn by middle-class women during the second half of the sixteenth century in an attempt to emulate French farthingales. This undergarment produced a much smaller and softer line over the hips as seen in the portrait of *Elizabeth Home (about 1599–1633), Countess of Suffolk*, about 1615–17 (fig. 50). John Chamberlain (1553–1627) in a letter to Dudley Carleton's wife Alice in February 1613 about the wedding of Princess Elizabeth Stuart (1596–1662) to Frederick V (1596–1632), Elector Palatine, wrote:

> One thing I had almost forgotten for hast that all this there was a course taken and so notified that no Lady or gentle-woman should be admitted to any of these sights with a verdingale, which was to gaine the more roome, and I hope may serve to make them quite left off in time.[12]

Lady Anne Clifford recalled in November 1617 that 'All the time I was at Court I wore my Green Damask Gown embroidered without a Farthingale'.[13]

At some stage in its subsequent history the petticoat was unpicked down the centre back seam with each half lined with brown tabby weave linen covered in light pink silk to form two panels. In the nineteenth century the two halves were sewn back together. During this later period at least one owner has carefully tried to replace some of the metal thread embroidery and spangles that had been lost over the centuries, using thin metal wire and small faceted steel beads. The latter became increasingly fashionable from the late 1850s after Sir Henry Bessemer (1813–98) patented a de-carbonization process for the mass manufacture of steel from pig iron in 1854, which made steel beads easier and cheaper to manufacture. The expanse of material in petticoats of the period would have made them easy to recycle into other garments or, more likely, domestic furnishings. It is lucky that this specific petticoat has survived with so little alteration.

---

12 McClure (1939), 65, cited in Vincent (2003), 37.
13 Clifford (1992), 64, cited in Vincent (2003), 35.

Gloves

Gloves were important accessories for both men and women. Their manufacture was a skilled trade, with the Worshipful Company of Glovers established by London glove makers in 1349. Although the Glovers were amalgamated with Pursers in 1498, they regained their independence by grant of Royal Charter from Charles I in 1638. Most gloves were made from fine kid leather that would have been expertly tanned and dressed. Gloves were not only practical for keeping hands clean and warm, they were also an easy way of showing the wearer's wealth and social status. An elaborately decorated pair of gloves signified that the wearer was rich, with ample servants to look after their person and household. In the first quarter of the seventeenth century it was fashionable to have fine leather gloves with embroidered gauntlet cuffs, as depicted in William Larkin's portrait of *Richard Sackville (1559–1624), 3rd Earl of Dorset*, 1613 (fig. 51). An inventory of Richard Sackville's wardrobe for 1617–19 lists several pairs of gloves, the majority embroidered to match specific outfits;

> [11] Item one paire of gloves with topps of Tissue in Coullors embroadered with Sonnes Moones and stares of gold …
> [19] Item one paire of gloves with topps of cloth of silver embroadered with globes flames and hartes of gold and laced with small gold lace' …
> [29] Item one paire of gloves with topps of tawney sattin embroad[ered] with gold and crimson silke and laced with gold lace …
> [39] Item one paire of gloves with topps of white cloth of siluer embroadered with slipps of black sattin and gold laced with gold and siluer lace …
> [56] Item one paire of gloves embroadered edged with gold and siluer lace …
> [67] Item one paire of gloves embroadered with gold and silver and edged with gold and silver …
> [102] Item one paire of gloves with topps of green sattin embroadered and edged wth gold lace …
> [125] Item one paire of gloues wth topps of Tawney sattin embrodered with gold and Crimson silke and laced with gold lace.[1]

1 Kent Archives Office, Sackville of Knole MSS (U269 E79/1), cited in Mactaggart (1980), 41–55.

Opposite Detail of fig. 52

Fig. 51: William Larkin, *Richard Sackville (1559–1624), 3rd Earl of Dorset*, 1613. Oil on canvas, 206.4 × 122.3 cm. English Heritage, Kenwood House, Suffolk Collection, London

Richard Sackville is depicted wearing an extravagant outfit with his gloves and shoes embroidered with black flowers outlined in gold to match his white doublet.

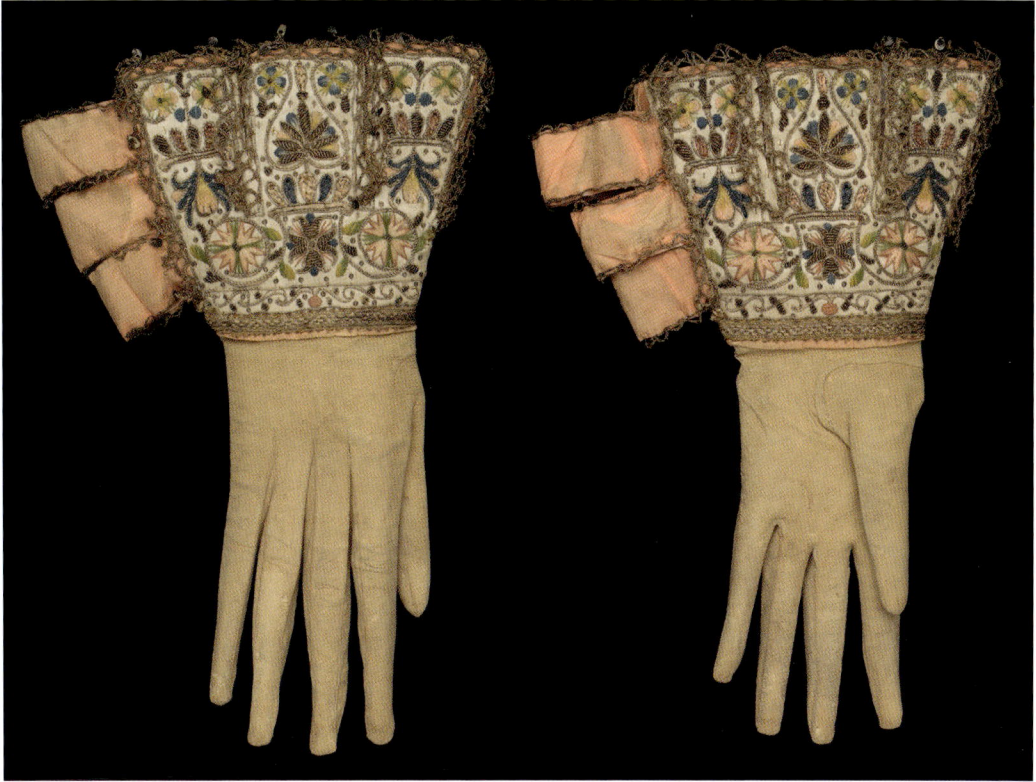

Fig. 52: Gloves, British, about 1610–30 (29.141.1–2)

The fingers of early seventeenth-century gloves were cut longer than required to produce a fashionable and elegant elongated line. Often it is still clear to see how far the fingers reached inside by where the soft kid has stretched compared to the tips.

The fashion for expensive gloves soon trickled down to the lower classes, as an Italian visitor to England in 1618 noted that 'All wear very costly gloves. This fashion for gloves is so universal that even the porters wear them ostentatiously'.[2] A pair of gloves, however costly, was one of the more economically accessible items of clothing that could be purchased in an attempt to emulate the fashions of the rich.

A pair of gloves has embroidered gauntlets made separately from the hand with six deep square-ended tabs (fig. 52). The ground, in white silk satin, is embroidered with blue, pink and yellow silk and silver-gilt threads in an arabesque design of stylized flowers and foliage embellished with regularly spaced silver-gilt spangles. They are further enhanced with an edge of silver-gilt bobbin lace decorated with spangles, which also edges the light pink silk ribbon loops at the opening. The inside of the cuffs are lined with matching pink silk that originally would have been a much brighter shade, but like most

2   Linthicum (1936), cited in Cunnington (1955), 74.

pink silks from the early–mid seventeenth century it has faded significantly. The gloves were previously in the collection of John Norton, 5th Baron Grantley (1855–1943).

Gloves were also given as gifts and tokens of fidelity, often scented with rosewater, jasmine oil, cloves, cumin or nutmeg. Queen Elizabeth I was presented with gloves when she visited Cambridge University in 1578;

> Also with the book the said Vice-chancellor presented a paire of gloves, perfumed and garnished with embroiderie and goldsmithe's wourke, price 60s … . In taking the book and gloves, it fortuned that the paper in which the gloves were folded to open; and hir Majestie behoulding the beautie of the said gloves, as in great admiration, and in token of hir thankfull acceptation of the same, held up one of hir hands.[3]

In particular, gloves were a popular choice for wedding or Valentine's Day gifts. During the seventeenth century it was customary to give a gift to the first person of the opposite sex seen on 14 February, St Valentine's Day. Given how expensive some of the gloves must have been it is unsurprising to learn that increasingly the gifting of gloves became by prior arrangement. Samuel Pepys, in his *Diary*, 18 February 1661 states that 'In the afternoon my wife and I and Mrs. Martha Batten, my Valentine, to the Exchange; and there, upon a payre of embroydered and six payre of plain white gloves I laid out 40s upon her.' Forty shillings in 1662 was the equivalent of eight months' wages for a maid.

Another pair of early seventeenth century gloves are also made of pale brown kid leather with an attached gauntlet with the upper section cut into six short square-ended tabs (fig. 53). The gauntlets of white silk satin are embroidered with silk and silver-gilt threads with a design of flowers, including pansies and borage, as well as knots and bullions. The gloves are further embellished with metal spangles and silver-gilt fringe around the tabs. These gloves appear to have been relatively well worn. Along the fingers additional long panels, known as forks, are inserted. However, there are no quarks, the tiny lozenge-shaped pieces that were sometimes fitted between each finger at the base to spread the strain. Without them this pair of gloves has suffered, and some of the seams at the bottom of the fingers have come apart.

3 Synge (1982). 39.

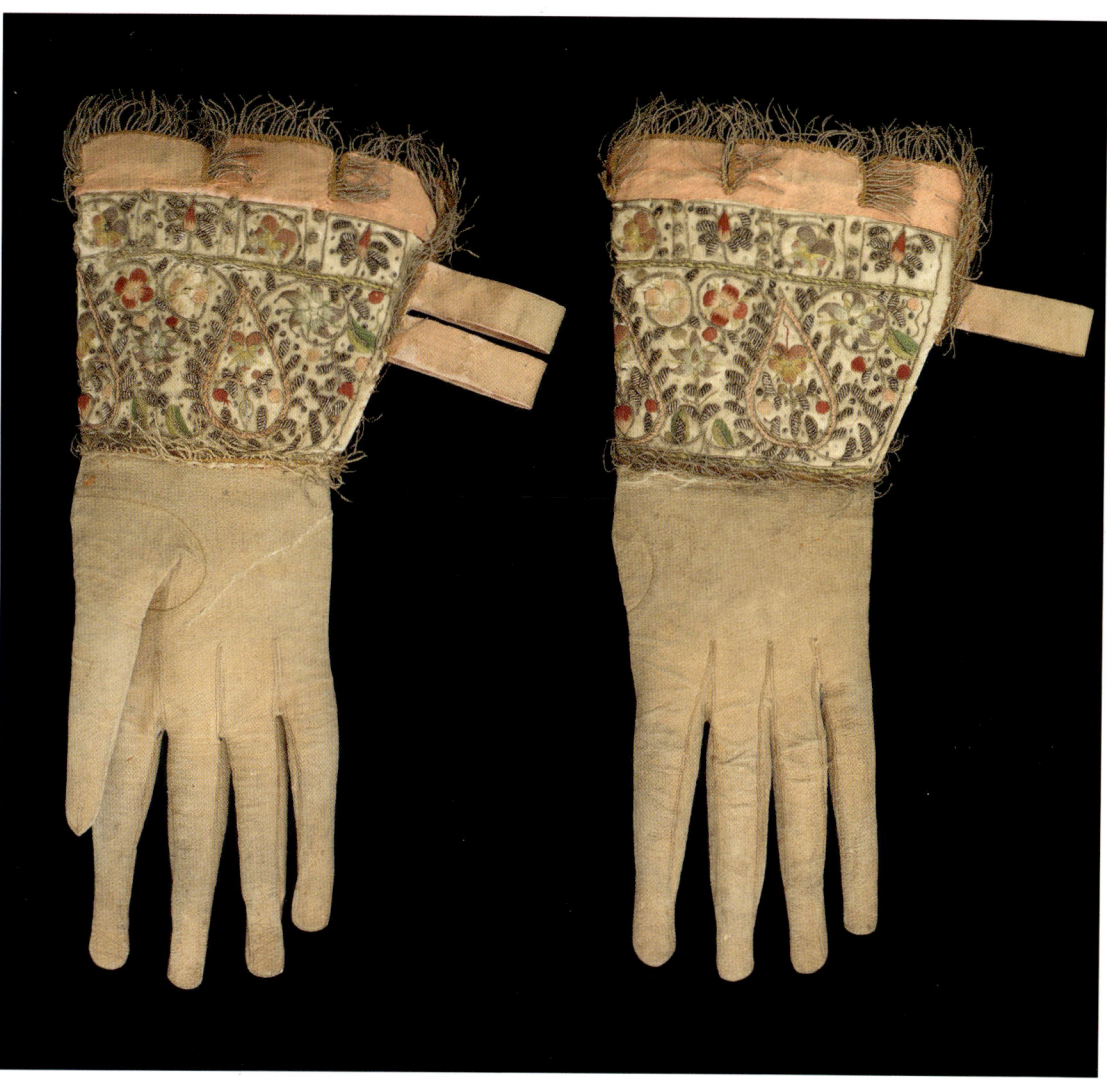

Fig. 53: Gloves, British, about 1610–30 (E.1971.111.a–b)
The flowers and leaves are embroidered predominantly in long-and-short and satin stitch. The outline of the design is worked in laid and couched silver-gilt thread.

Falconry Accessories

Falconry originated in central Asia in approximately 2,000 BC; one of the earliest depictions of the sport is on an Assyrian bas-relief at Khorsabad dating to 1,722–5 BC. It arrived in Britain during the ninth century AD and became a regular pastime for royals and aristocrats. Harold II (about 1022–66) is shown with a falcon on the late eleventh-century embroidered Bayeaux Tapestry. However, the first royal mews to house birds of prey was not built until the reign of Richard II (1367–1400). When it was later burnt down in 1537 Henry VIII had a larger mews built in west London on the site that is now the National Gallery.

A fantastic example of a set of falconry accessories includes a glove with matching pouch, a lure and two hoods. As falcons are flown from the hand rather than a perch one of the most important accessories is a glove which extends over the wrist and lower arm to protect the wearer from the long, sharp talons of the bird. Randle Holme, in *Academy of*

Fig. 54: Falconry glove, British, early 17th century (29.151.2)

Both the mistletoe and bramble are used as talismanic symbols. The first often represents life and male fertility, whilst the latter, known as the 'blessed bramble' in the Scottish highlands, was used both literally and symbolically for its healing properties.

Opposite Detail of fig. 60

Armoury, 1688, describes 'a thick, strong glove, with a Button and Tassell at the lower part of it, on which he carrieth his Hawk to secure his hand from her Tallons'.[1] The glove is not only beneficial to the wearer but also the falcon, as it provides a wider, easier perch for the bird to grip. Traditionally the glove is worn on the left hand as it was customary to go hunting on horseback, and riders often use their stronger right hand to hold the horse's reins. The tassel hanging from the lower point of the gauntlet was not only a decorative feature, but was used to secure the falcon on the hand with thin leather ties, known as jesses, whilst travelling to and from the hunt. This glove is made from reddish-brown leather with the gauntlets embroidered in multicoloured silk, silver and silver-gilt threads with intertwining mistletoe and brambles (figs. 54 and 55).

1 Cunnington and Mansfield (1969), 182.

Fig. 55: Detail of embroidered gauntlet in fig. 54

The wide u-shaped mistletoe is embroidered on the lower half of the gauntlet with yellow silk thread with straight and coiled silver-gilt threads couched over with the outline in coiled metal plate, known as smooth purl. The upper half of the gauntlet is covered with brambles. The flowers are in white silk thread embroidered in burden stitch over flat metal plate, which can be clearly seen on some petals where the silk has worn away. The bramble stems are worked in couched metal threads. The blackberries are again worked in a variety of different ways, with some made from smooth purl.

Fig. 56: Tapestry, *Falconry*, Flemish, about 1475 (46.61)

The huntsman on the left aiming his cross-bow wears a blue pouch with a gold clasp hanging from his belt. Other falconry equipment is depicted in the tapestry, including a glove worn by the kneeling man.

Fig. 57: Falconry pouch, British, early 17th century (29.151.1)

A tree provides the central point to the embroidery design, the trunk of which is worked with rows of untwisted silk thread, each wrapped in a spiral with a metal thread. The green mound from which the tree and brambles grow is embroidered in burden stitch.

Falconry Accessories 85

Pouches, a form of bag, were hung from the falconer's belt and carried spare jesses and small pieces of meat to feed the falcon with when training and hunting (fig. 56). A pouch, made to match the glove, is embroidered with the same design of mistletoe and brambles (fig. 57). It is constructed in two sections that are joined at the top by a hinged gold mount, the shaft of the hinge passing through a plaque surmounted by a looped ring, used to suspend the pouch from the belt (fig. 58). The gold is enamelled in green, white,

Fig. 58: Detail of enamelled gold hinged mount in fig. 57

The central section of each half of the pouch forms a pocket, lined with silk, accessible by the opening within a gold enamelled mount that closes with a tasselled cord gold-plaited drawstring edged with gold fringe. Additional pockets are positioned inside the two halves of the pouch.

86 *Seventeenth-century Costume*

Fig. 59: Attributed to John Scougall after Paul van Somer, *George Heriot*, 1698. Oil on canvas, 127 × 95.25 cm. George Heriot Trust, Edinburgh

Heriot was appointed goldsmith to Anne of Denmark in 1597 and subsequently to James VI and I in 1601. After the accession of James VI to the English throne in 1603, he moved down to London where he was one of three jewellers to the King with a salary of £150 per annum.

Fig. 60: Tapestry, *Fight between a Falcon and a Heron*, French, about 1525 (46.60)

The lure in use by the falconer on the left looks as if it is trimmed with feathers to resemble a bird in flight.

yellow and black with brambles to match the embroidery. Like the high quality of the embroidery on these items, the enamel work is of exceptionally high standard and undoubtedly professional work. One possibility is that it was made by George Heriot (1563–1624) (fig. 59).

Another falconry accessory was the lure, a u-shaped weight attached to the end of a cord that was used as a

Fig. 61: Lure, British, early 17th century (29.151.3)

The tufts of blue silk and metal threads on the horns of the lure may have had feathers attached to them originally. The eight short braids hanging from the middle of the lure would have produced a whistling sound to attract the bird's attention.

Falconry Accessories

Fig. 62a

Fig. 62b

Figs. 62a and 62b: Falconry hoods, British, late 16th and early 17th centuries (29.151.4–5)

These hoods, known as Dutch hoods, are made in three sections and were shaped to fit on wooden blocks. The two plain hoods have sides in wool. The third hood, made before 1603, is more decorative, made with silk velvet panels edged with silver-gilt trim.

90 *Seventeenth-century Costume*

Fig. 63: Attributed to Rowland Lockey, after Arnold van Bronckorst, *James VI of Scotland (1566–1625)*, 1574. Oil on canvas, 118 × 73 cm. National Portrait Gallery, London

The Boke of St Albans, 1485, listed the hierarchy of raptors together with notes on which were to be used by each rank of society. At the top was the peregrine (*Falco peregrinus*), which, along with kestrels, merlins and hobbies, is one of four types of falcons native to the British Isles. With a wingspan of 95–115cm the peregrine was the largest falcon in Britain during this period. Once it targets its prey the bird descends, folding its wings to produce a more aerodynamic shape and then beating them to accelerate up to 240mph, making it the fastest species in the world. It is unsurprising that peregrines were restricted for use by royalty only.

prey substitute when training young falcons and to recall birds in flight back to the hand (fig. 60). A horseshoe-shaped wooden lure is covered in blue silk, silver and silver gilt thread braid (fig. 61). Today this style of lure is less favoured as falcons risk hitting them too hard during flight and injuring themselves, due to the speed of their flight.

Falconry Accessories 91

Fig. 64: Wroxton Abbey, Oxfordshire. Fairleigh Dickinson University

Wroxton Abbey is built on the site of a thirteenth-century Augustinian priory that had been left in disrepair after the Dissolution of the Monasteries in 1536. The current building was begun by Sir William Pope in 1618, just prior to James VI and I's visit.

Several falconry accessories (fig. 62) belonged to James VI and I, an avid falconer from an early age, as shown in a painting of a young monarch with one of his peregrines, attributed to Rowland Lockey, after Arnold van Bronckorst, *James VI of Scotland*, 1574 (fig. 63). James is said to have left these items behind, presumably as prerequisites, during a visit to Wroxton Abbey in Oxfordshire (fig. 64). When Burrell purchased them in 1934 it was recorded that the king had been visiting Lord Dudley North, 3rd Baron North (1581–1666), to act as godfather to one of his children. However, in the early seventeenth century Wroxton Abbey was the property of Sir William Pope (1573–1631). Pope was a popular courtier in the Jacobean court, whom James VI and I visited at Wroxton Abbey on 23 August 1619. During his brief stay the monarch was entertained 'with fashionable and courtly diversions of hawking and bear baiting'.[2] Sir William Pope commemorated the Royal visit by commissioning a stained

2 Nichols (1828), 563.

glass panel for the abbey, inscribed '*Icy dans cette chambre coucha nostre Roy Jacques, premier de nom, le 23me Aoust 1619*' (Here in this chamber slept our King James, first of that name, 23 August 1619). Pope remained in favour with James and was later raised to the Irish peerage as 1st Earl of Downe on 16 October 1628. Two generations later the abbey passed to the North family after Frances Pope, granddaughter of Sir William Pope, married Francis North (1637–1685), 1st Baron Guildford, the grandson of the aforementioned Lord Dudley North. The falconry accessories passed by descent though the family until they were acquired by the collector Percival D. Griffiths (about 1862–1937) of Castle Hedingham, Essex, in the early twentieth century.

This group of falcon accoutrements is completed with two hoods (see fig. 62a). As falcons are often taken hunting in groups, hoods are worn to blind the falcons when on the handler's arm allowing them to rest without distraction or excitement as they take it in turns to be flown. The feather plumes at the top of each of the hoods are not only for decoration, but also allowed the handler to easily remove the hood without injuring the bird's eyes. Another larger and more decorative falconry hood (see fig. 62b) was purchased by Sir William Burrell in 1938. Burrell's Purchase Book records that '[t]he hood is much larger than was usual and was evidently made for an important person. Only the very highest nobility were allowed to use very big hawks and this hood was made for a big falcon.' The leather central panel has been stamped with various motifs, including Tudor Roses, which suggests that this hood may have been used by Elizabeth I, who was also a keen falconer like her younger cousin.

Another decorative hood was made in southern Germany or Italy in the late seventeenth century (fig. 65). A design has been scored into the leather central panel, whilst the silk sides are embroidered with stylized flowers and leaves in silver-gilt threads. The glove is of heavy buff leather with an over-gauntlet that wraps over to provide additional protection to the wearer and support to the falcon. It is an exact match to a falconer's glove in the Bayerisches-National Museum, Munich.[3] It was acquired together with a falcon's hood, with the block sides decorated with metal thread embroidery.

---

3 Bayerisches-National Museum, Munich, T 6607. Illustrated in Borkopp-Restle (2002) 65.

These two items were purchased with two other objects originally catalogued as falconry accessories. One is a leather purse constructed with a central pouch surrounded by four smaller pockets, each closing with a drawstring. It is very similar to an example in the Bayerisches-National Museum, which is identified as a woman's money bag from the late sixteenth-century.[4] The fourth item consists of a drawstring pouch attached to a long panel with metal plates. It was possibly an accessory for a hunting rifle, to contain bullets and carry powder containers.

4 Bayerisches-National Museum, Munich, T 4443. Illustrated in Pietsch (2013) 48.

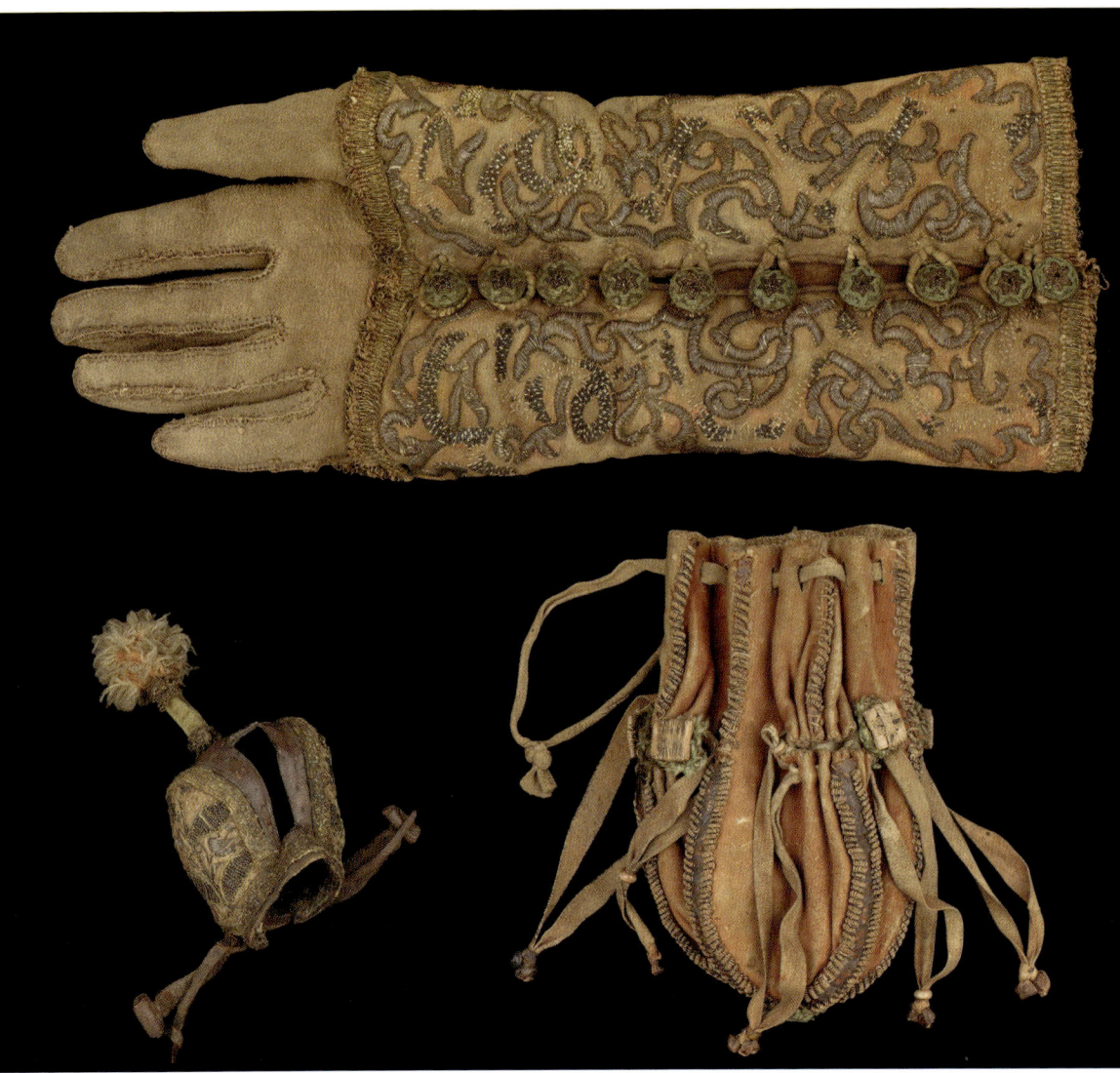

Fig. 65: Falconry glove and hood with bag and hunting accessory, late 16th – late 17th centuries (29.152.1–4)

The wrap-around gauntlet on the glove is embroidered with padded metal thread in an arabesque design, edged in gilt braid and fastened with ten silk and metal wrapped buttons.

Falconry Accessories

Bags

Small decorative bags or purses appear on many late sixteenth and seventeenth-century household inventories, often listed as 'sweet bags'. The inventory taken after the death of Henry Howard (1540–1614), 1st Earl of Northampton, lists the contents of each room together with their monetary value. Several sweet bags were in the higher library, including;

> Item two verie large sweet bagges embrodred with embosted worke of silver, gold, and coulored silkes, and filled upp with ovals of divers personages, lined both with clowded sattenes black the ground white … 15 li
> Item a smaller sweet bagge embrodered with high embosted mosseworke having two sea nymphs upon dolphins and other figures of fowles, edged about with lace of silver and gold, lined with carnation … 20 s
> Item a white taffeta sweet bagge with couloured flowers in ovals of gold, laced with carnacion … 20 s
> Item one large cloth of silver sweet bagge embrodered with pinched plate of golde lined with russett Taffata … 20 s
> Item one large white satten sweet bagge embrodered with knottes of silver Oes with burning hartes … 25 s
> Item one large white satten sweet bagge embrodered with a runninge worke of roses and flowers in silke and golde, lined with a striped silver Grogeran … 30 s
> Item a carnacion taffta sweet bagge embrodered with a twist of silver on both sides … 10 s
> Item a small white satten sweet bagge embrodered with flies wormes and flowers in silke and golde … 20 s
> …
> Item one small sweet bagge of Tent work the ground silver with pottes and flowers lined with greene sattin … 6 s 8 d[1]

'Oes' was another word for metal spangles, the forerunner of today's plastic sequins.

Again, another inventory taken at Denmark House after the death of Anne of Denmark in 1619 includes a large number of sweet bags;

> One Sweete bagg of white Tincell embrodered wth silke. …
> A sweete bagg of white satten embrodered.
> Another sweete bagg of white saten wth knots of silver. …

1 Shirley (1869), 362–369, cited in Carey (2009), 21.

Opposite Detail of fig. 68

A sweete bagg of Seaworke wrought wth gold silver & coulored silke & lined wth greene taffata.
A sweete bagg of white cloth of silver embrodered wth gold & silver & coluored silke wth an Owle on each Corner on both sides & lined wth Carnacon taffata.
A sweete bag of cloth of silver embroderd round about the border wth gold silver & coulored silke & lined wth Cloth of silver striped wth gold & orringe coulor taffata wthin. …
Two very riche swette bags of white satten embrodered wth gold and silke of sondry Coulors wth the arms of England on one of them …
A Carpett sweete bag …
A sweete bagg of white satten embrodered.
A sweete bagg the ground watchett satten embrodered wth divers pictures and lined wth Carnacon satten. …
A sweete bagg of white sateen and lined wth Carnacon and peachcoulor taffata.
A small sweete bag embrodered.[2]

The main use for these exquisitely embroidered bags was to be filled with fragrant herbs or perfumed powders. These were placed in linen and clothes closets, much like lavender bags today. K. Platt, writing in *Delightes for Ladies, to adorn their Persons, Tables, Closets, and distillatories*, 1602, includes an example of a typical recipe;

> 35 Sweet bags to lie among linen.
> Fill your bags only with lignum Rhodium finely beaten, and it will give an excellent sent to your linnen.[3]

Gervaise Markham, *Country Contentments, or The English Huswife*, 1615, has instructions for a more complex fragrance;

> To make sweete powder for bagges.
> Take of Arras six ounces, of Damaske rose-leaves as much, of Margerom and sweete Basill, of each an ounce, of Cloves two ounces, yellow Saunders two ounces, of Citron pills seven drams, of Lignum-aloes, one ounce, of Benjamine one ounce, of Storaxe one ounce, of Muske one dram: bruise all these and put them into a bagge of silke or linnen, but silke is the best.[4]

Another option was to wear such bags on the person suspended from a girdle around the waist. Several sweet bags have survived with pin cushions attached, which would have

2 Payne (2001), 23–44.
3 Carey (2009), 9.
4 Carey (2009), 8.
5 Gallery of Costume, Manchester 1984.60.

Fig. 66: Sweet bag, British, about 1600–30 (29.155)

The sweet bag was made from a long rectangle of plain weave linen that, once embroidered, was folded in half and the outside edges seamed to form the small square bag. The floral motifs are embroidered in silk threads worked in tent stitch, whilst the silver thread background is in Gobelin stitch. At the top the loops show where the drawstring, now missing, would have been threaded through and at the bottom are three small tassels.

been hung together with other small items such as needlework tools and small books on or in the same manner as a chatelaine, a clasp worn suspended from a woman's waist with useful tools attached. A set consisting of a sweet bag, pin cushion and knife case in crimson red silk satin embroidered with silver and silver-gilt threads is in the Gallery of Costume, Manchester.[5] Whilst several sweet bags do survive in museum collections, it is surprising that there are not a great deal more, given the high number of bags listed in the inventories of the period. The majority that do exist have similar characteristics. They are often fairly small – in a square shape about 10–12cm long and wide, closed with a drawstring along the top edge, and are decorated with tassels (figs. 66 and 67).

Bags 99

Fig. 67: Reverse of sweet bag in fig. 66

Most sweet bags have very similar patterns on their front and reverse sides. On this example the design is slightly different on the two sides, with flowers on both sides, but a bird on only one.

Another use for these bags was as purses to hold money or jewellery that could be given or presented on important occasions, such as those given to the monarch by bishops and the higher levels of the aristocracy at New Year. Henry Hastings (1586–1643), 5th Earl of Huntingdon, describes making his gift in 1604–5;

> The manner of presenting a New Year's gift to his Majesty from the Earl of Huntingdon. You must buy a new purse of about Vs. price, and put thereinto 20 pieces of new gold of 20s. apiece, and go to the Presence-Chamber, where the Court is, upon New Year's day, in the morning about 8 o'clock, and deliver the purse and the gold unto my Lord Chamberlain....[6]

---

6 Nichols (1828), I, 471, cited in Arnold (1988), 93.

100   *Seventeenth-century Costume*

Fig. 68: Sweet bag, British, about 1600–30 (29.310)

The flowers are sewn in detached buttonhole stitch with the petals combining shaded coloured silk threads and metal threads. The centres of three flowers are worked in coiled metal strips, known as purl, and the small leaves are in tent stitch. The whole is offset against a silver ground of brick stitch. The open edge along the top of the bag closes with a drawstring of plaited pink silk and silver-wrapped threads that are decorated at the ends with matching tassels. Along the bottom are three red silk tassels, their loops covered in metal purl. Inside the bag is lined with pink silk.

Fig. 69: Detail of embroidered cornflower in fig. 68

Cornflowers (*Centaurea cyanus*) have been used to symbolize reliability and fidelity. Young men in love, who believed that if the blue flower faded fast their feelings were not reciprocated, wore them.

The majority of surviving sweet bags were made by professional embroiderers, whilst silk workers specializing in narrow wares and trimmings would have made the braids and tassels. Another sweet bag is very similar to examples in the British Museum, London, and the Victoria and Albert Museum, London (fig. 68).[7] This suggests that these bags were created ready to be purchased for such occasions as the New Year's gifts.[8] The *rinceau* design is regularly arranged in a cinquefoil pattern with the scrolling stems worked using silver-gilt thread in plaited braid stitch. The design, which incorporates borage, carnation, eglantine rose and cornflower, is repeated on both sides of the bag (fig. 69). This lavish style of embroidery with a ground of brick stitch is also found on the early seventeenth-century Devereux bodice that is thought to have belonged to Frances Walsingham (1567–1633), Countess of Essex and Clanricarde, wife of Robert Devereux (1565–1601), 2nd Earl of Essex, that is now in the Kyoto Costume Institute.[9]

7 British Museum 1866,0627.146, Victoria and Albert Museum T.248-1960.
8 Victoria and Albert Museum, T.248–1960.
9 Kyoto Costume Institute AC6328 89–16.
10 Victoria and Albert Museum, 4062–1856, 522–1869, 1119–1869 and T.20–1939.

Fig. 70: Bag, British, late 17th century (29.154)

The bag is constructed from four panels of silk, embroidered in dark and light green silk thread with two designs of stylized flowers and geometric motifs in rococo stitch. The seams are edged with dark green silk and it fastens with a silk ribbon drawstring around the top of the bag.

One larger bag dates to the final quarter of the century (fig. 70). It is not known specifically what this style of round drawstring bag may have contained. Smaller, circular purses with stiffened bases and wide drawstring openings at the top were popular for holding coins or tokens for gambling. These were designed to sit on the table with their aperture wide enough to easily access coins during the course of the game. Some examples which survive in the Victoria and Albert Museum are embroidered with their owners' initials or coat of arms so that they could be easily distinguished from other gamblers' purses.[10] However this bag is larger, with a less rigid structure to its construction. Its wide drawstring opening suggests that it may have been a work bag used to hold sewing threads and other needlework accessories.

Knitted Waistcoat

Knitting is thought to have originated in the Middle East, and it was first used in Europe by the Moors of Spain in the thirteenth century. Surviving examples of early knitting are made using solely knit stitch, with purl stitch not appearing until the middle of the sixteenth century.[1] Knitted garments made during this period ranged from wool caps for working men, to silk stockings for the aristocracy. During Elizabeth I's reign knitting became popular, not only with professionals, who were taught at specialist schools, but also with amateurs at home. An early knitting frame was invented by William Lee (about 1550–1614) in around 1589–1600. However, it does not appear to have gone into commercial use.[2] Later frames were developed during the seventeenth century, but these could only produce up to eight stitches per inch, in comparison with 13 to 20 stitches by hand.[3]

One of the earliest types of knitted garments to survive in museum collections is waistcoats. Both men and women wore these items of clothing either as undergarments during the day or as *déshabillé* at home in the evening to provide additional warmth. These items tend to fall into two categories: Italian waistcoats that open down the front, sometimes known as Florentine waistcoats, and those that pulled over the head. Italian waistcoats were knitted using one or two colours of silk yarn, in imitation of patterns found on woven silks, the effect often enhanced with the use of purl stitches. The fine gauge of these waistcoats suggests that they were hand-knitted in professional workshops, using extremely fine metal knitting needles, known as 'wires', for wealthy classes to buy as ready-to-wear clothing (fig. 71). The garment is constructed from rectangular knitted sections; two front panels, two back panels and two sleeves. Several have triangular gores inserted to provide additional width over the hips, at home by the wearer or a member of their household. Their name suggests that they were made in Italy and exported to northern Europe, but it is now known that fine silk yarns were imported from Naples to London from the late sixteenth century to supply the native knitting industry.[4]

1 Rutt (1987), 64.
2 Hart and North (1998), 184.
3 Pulliam (2002), 173.
4 Hart and North (1998), 184.

Opposite Detail of waistcoat in fig. 71

Fig. 71: Waistcoat, possibly British or Italian, about 1600–20 with later alterations (29.126)

The border around the hips was worked in garter stitch with the scalloped edge formed by stretching the knitting, rather than in adding stitches to create the points.[5]

[5] Unpublished correspondence with Ruth Gilbert, 2006 in Glasgow Museums' Archives.

Fig. 72: Detail of knitting in fig. 71

The metal thread is made from a yellow silk two-ply core that is S-twist (diagonally from top right to bottom left) loosely wrapped with a narrow strip of silver-gilt metal to reveal partially the yellow silk below. It is knitted approximately 14 stitches per inch.

Figures 71 and 72 depict a waistcoat hand-knitted in a beige two-ply silk and silver-gilt thread with the geometric pattern created not only with the two colours but also by alternating the front and back face of the stocking stitch. Originally the waistcoat would have been made in a flat-cut T-shape created from rectangular panels and may have been lined (fig. 73).

Later in the century, or possibly at the beginning of the eighteenth century, the waistcoat has been re-made by cutting up the rectangular panels as if they were a woven textile and re-seaming them to create a more fitted jacket to suit the contemporary fashion. In contrast with the fine gauge of the initial knitting, these later alternations are very amateurish. They include widening and lowering the décolletage by cutting off the original high, round neckline. The new edge does not have a sewn hem, but is simply folded back and gummed down. The body is no longer square, but fitted with a short flared peplum formed by

Fig. 73: Waistcoat, possibly British or Italian, about 1600–20. Silk and silver-gilt yarn, centre-back 57 cm. Victoria and Albert Museum, London

This is knitted using stocking, reverse stocking and basket weave stitches in blue and yellow silk yarns spiral wrapped in silver foil. It fastens at the front with passementerie buttons.

cutting and tailoring the garment. The new seams are sewn in relatively large running stitches using a loosely twisted silk thread and the cut edges are left unbound and fraying. The sleeves were knitted in the round, but with a plain narrow line running down the length in imitation of sleeves made from woven cloth that have a seam. Originally full-length, the sleeves were removed, shortened and reset as part of the alterations. Fullness was created at the top by gathering them into the shoulder and they were tapered to the wrist to fasten with four or five buttons, which are now missing. There is evidence from symmetrical crease lines that there may have been a dart on each of the front panels to further reduce the size of the waist, but these were unpicked before the waistcoat was acquired by Sir William Burrell from John Hunt (1900–1976). Intriguingly it is the only knitted item in his collection.

Because knitted waistcoats were for informal wear there are no known sources showing them being worn, making it hard to give them a more specific date. They appear to have originated at the beginning of the seventeenth century. Lady Howard ordered 'a pound of woosted for wastecotes' for 9 shillings in 1618 and the Danish Royal family used knitted silk waistcoats for children's shrouds during this period.[6]

Knitted waistcoats continued to be worn throughout the century. There are records of waistcoats being relined during the course of their use. Sir Thomas Islam is billed £1 5s 6d from his tailor for 'new Lining A Purple and gold Silke knit wastcoate' in April 1680.[7] There are continuing references to them also in the early eighteenth century, including a London newspaper report of the theft of a 'green silk knit waistcoat with gold and silver flowers all over it' in 1712.[8] The later alterations to the waistcoat in the Burrell Collection certainly attest to their continued use.

---

6 North and Tiramani (eds) (2011), 88.
7 Transcript of the Islam Bills, John Lea Nevinson Archives, Victoria and Albert Museum, London, cited in North and Tiramani (eds) (2011), 88.
8 Rothstein (1984), 18.

Items Associated with Charles II and Oliver Cromwell

The middle of the seventeenth century was a turbulent time with the Wars of the Three Kingdoms in England, Scotland and Ireland (1639–51) as the crown, churches and parliaments fought over differing religious and political ideologies. As a result of these troubles it is understandable that fewer items of costume survive from this period than from earlier and later in the century. Two groups of items dating from the 1640s are interesting, but not necessarily of high technical or decorative value when compared with other examples of seventeenth-century costume collected by Sir William Burrell. However, both sets are historically associated with key figures in the English Civil War; namely Charles, Prince of Wales and later Charles II, and Oliver Cromwell, later Lord Protector. Today it is hard to provide empirical proof that these items did have such illustrious owners in the 1640s, but it is probably because of these stories that the objects were kept safe during the subsequent centuries and why they were collected.

The first group comprises a nightcap with matching slippers and a quilted waistcoat. Burrell's Purchase Book for 1937 records them as;

> A cap, tunic and shoes worn by Charles II when as Prince of Wales in 1645 he was sent to take charge of the Royalist forces in the West of England … on this occasion Charles stayed in the house of Colonel Thomas Veel of Alverstone near Bristol and left these things as a souvenir of his visit. They have been handed down in the family & have recently been purchased from a direct descendant.[1]

Charles first accompanied his father during the wars at the Battle of Edgehill on 23 October 1642 (fig. 74). Three years later, aged only 15, Charles was made titular General of the Western Association. He and his army left Oxford on 4 March 1645 accompanied by Lord Arthur Capel and Sir Ralph Hopton (1596–1652), initially staying in Bridgwater and later in Bristol. They were defeated by General Thomas Fairfax (1612–71) and the New Model Army at the Battle of Langport on 10 July, who later stormed Bristol on 10 September.[2]

Opposite Detail of fig. 78

---

1 Purchase Book 1937, 36–37 in Glasgow Museums' Archives.
2 Seaward (2004).

Fig. 74: William Dobson, *Charles II when Prince of Wales*, about 1642. Oil on canvas, 153.6 × 129.8 cm. Scottish National Portrait Gallery

The young prince is depicted in semi-military dress. Over his fashionable silk doublet and breeches he wears a thick buff coat and cuirass (armour covering his chest) whilst the page holds his helmet.

The nightcap has a much shorter crown than those from the beginning of the century and is made from eight conical panels of salmon pink silk satin (fig. 75). Each section would have been embroidered with the same formalized pattern, possibly a stylized pineapple, worked in silver and silver-gilt threads before the nightcap was made up (fig. 76). Once constructed, the seams between the sections were overlaid with lines of twisted silver thread

Fig. 75: Nightcap, British, about 1640–60 (29.133)

The silver and silver-gilt threads are laid in loops and couched in place with fine silk thread. The pattern is further embellished with appliquéd beads and spangles sewn in the spaces on the silk ground.

Fig. 76: Detail of pineapple in fig. 75

The main motif may be a stylized pineapple. The pineapple, which is indigenous to South America, was first introduced to Europe from Guadeloupe by Christopher Columbus (1451–1506) in 1493.

Items associated with Charles II and Oliver Cromwell 113

and a lining of yellow plain-weave silk was added. The pair of slippers have the silk vamps (the panel over the front of the foot) embroidered to match (fig. 77). The quality and uniformity of the embroidery suggests that they were made by a professional. Round toes had been fashionable at the turn of the century, but by the 1620s a squarer profile was becoming popular. The nightcap and slippers would have been worn as *déshabillé* on informal, private occasions.

The man's waistcoat is made from quilted pinkish-red satin (fig. 78). It is flat-cut with long panels for the front and back of the body with tapering skirts to the upper thigh and it fastens at the centre front with 25 silk-covered buttons. The long sleeves, cut with a slight curve at the elbows, taper to the wrist where they fasten with four buttons. It is beautifully made with fine, even hand-stitching and all the seams are finished with narrow silk braid bindings. However, unlike the doublets of the period that were cut with a waist seam between the upper body panels and skirt, this waistcoat is a very unusual cut for its attributed date, with its long body panels that are cut in one piece from collar to hip. One other waistcoat with a similar cut made of fine cream wool is in the Victoria and Albert Museum, and is another rare undergarment to survive from

Fig. 77: Slippers, British, about 1640–60 (29.144–145)

The slippers, like many heeled shoes at this period, were made on straight lathes. Neither the silk vamps nor the leather soles are cut to fit the curved insteps of left and right feet.

Fig. 78: Waistcoat, British, about 1640–80 (29.128)
The silk is backed with wool and linen and quilted with narrow parallel rows of zig-zag lines sewn in pinkish-red silk thread worked in neat, even running stitches. Originally it was lined with plain-weave pink silk, but this has deteriorated over the centuries leaving only remnants around the buttonholes.

Fig. 79: Anthony van Dyck, *William Feilding, 1st Earl of Denbigh*, about 1633–34. Oil on canvas, 247.5 × 148.5 cm. National Gallery, London

William Feilding was the brother-in-law of Charles Villiers, Duke of Buckingham, one of Charles I's most noted favourites. He travelled to Persia and India in 1631–33.

this period.[3] It is believed that this cut for main garments was not introduced until Charles II first wore his vest, the forerunner of the coat, in 1666. However, there are notable precedents for men's upper garments not having a waist seam, such as the buff coats worn by the cavalrymen that have the body panels cut in one piece with the skirts. A more exotic example is depicted by Anthony van Dyck in his portrait *William Feilding (about 1582–1643), 1st Earl of Denbigh*, about 1633–34 (fig. 79) in which the sitter is shown wearing a Hindu pyjama suit that he presumably brought back as a souvenir of his time in India.

As discussed in the previous chapter, waistcoats were worn as undergarments to provide additional warmth. As a result, there are no known depictions in portraits or paintings of the period with which to verify the cut with the date. James Master's *Expense Book* for 1649–50 includes entries 'For three yds. of watchet sattin to make me a waistcoat at £1.13.0.' and 'For making my sattin waistcoat & my great coat £1.15.0.'.[4] Several years later, after the Restoration, Samuel Pepys, writing in his *Diary*, 20 June 1666 includes the statement 'I have of late taken too much cold by washing my feet and going in a thin silke waistcoate, without any other coate over it, and open breasted'. Another possibility is that the quilted silk waistcoat was a very late form of gambeson – a padded defensive jacket – designed to be put on under the buff coats worn by wealthy aristocratic combatants in the Civil Wars.

It is impossible to state categorically whether Charles II wore these items. The nightcap, slippers and waistcoat are relatively small for a man. However, Charles was only 15 in 1645 so the provenance cannot be ruled out on physical attributes alone. The provenance states the clothing was given to Thomas Veel (about 1591–1663/4) as a souvenir of a visit, presumably as a prerequisite. Veel was born at Alveston, Gloucestershire, the younger son of Nicholas Veel. During the English Civil War he fought as a Royalist army officer, was named Royalist Commission of the Peace in March 1643 and appointed governor of Berkeley Castle in November of that year. Although he was dismissed from that role in August 1644, he remained in arms in the West Country until at least June 1645, so there is a possibility that he may have met, if not hosted, Charles during the campaign. Veel continued to serve the Royalist cause

3 Victoria and Albert Museum, T.148–1937. With thanks to David Wilcox for drawing my attention to this waistcoat.
4 *Archeologia Cantiana* vols. XV, XVI, XVII, XVIII, cited in Cunnington (1955), 24.

during the Commonwealth, raising men in preparation for Charles II's proposed landing in 1656. Sir Edward Massey (about 1619–74) spent several months hiding at Veel's family house at Symondshall in 1659 while organizing his revolt, leading to Massey, Veel and his male relatives being arrested on 31 July and the Veel estates being sequestered. Evidence suggests that there may have been some form of personal connection between Charles II and Veel during the conflicts as several attempts were made after the Restoration to reward Thomas Veel. Whilst these were not successful before his death, his descendants were later rewarded by Charles when he granted Veel's son, Nicholas, and grandson, Thomas, the office of making and registering assurances in London.[5] A more pragmatic possibility is that the items originally belonged to Thomas Veel.

Numerous items in museum collections have historic attributions to key figures from the past, often with little or no evidence. Costume often acquires romantic associations, probably because articles of clothing are worn and therefore have been physically very close to a person. This is particularly true of a pair of gloves and nightcap said to have belonged to Oliver Cromwell. Sir William Burrell's Purchase Book for 1937 includes a quotation from an undated newspaper cutting stating that;

> These dainty __ Noll left behind him at Chard when he retreated before the advancing army of Charles I in July, 1645 .... They were placed in a Chard church vault, where they stayed until two years ago, when the owner of the vault gave them away to settle a debt.[6]

Unfortunately, recent research has not provided any evidence to authenticate the attribution. Oliver Cromwell was in the West Country during 1645. He fought in the Battle of Naseby, Northamptonshire, on 14 June, and then in the Battle of Langport, Somerset, on 10 July. It is known that he was also involved in sieges at Bridgwater, Sherbourne, Bristol, Devizes and Winchester, however, no specific reference to a visit to Chard in Somerset has been found.[7]

The gloves are made of light brown kid leather with stylized birds and tulips embroidered on the gauntlets (figs. 80 and 81). This design and embroidery techniques are similar to those found on several other pairs of gloves, including a pair said to have belonged to James VI and I.[8]

5 Warmington (2004).
6 Purchase Book, 1937, 49.
7 Morrill (2004).
8 Metropolitan Museum Rogers Fund, by exchange, 1923, 29.23.13,14. Morrall and Watt (2008), 126–7. Attribution first asserted by Redfern, *Royal and Historic Gloves and Shoes* (1904), 31.
9 On loan from the Worshipful Company of Glovers to the Fashion Museum, Bath, 23362a and Lady Lever Art Gallery, Port Sunlight, LL5412 (X3383).
10 Gallery of Costume, Manchester 1972.55.

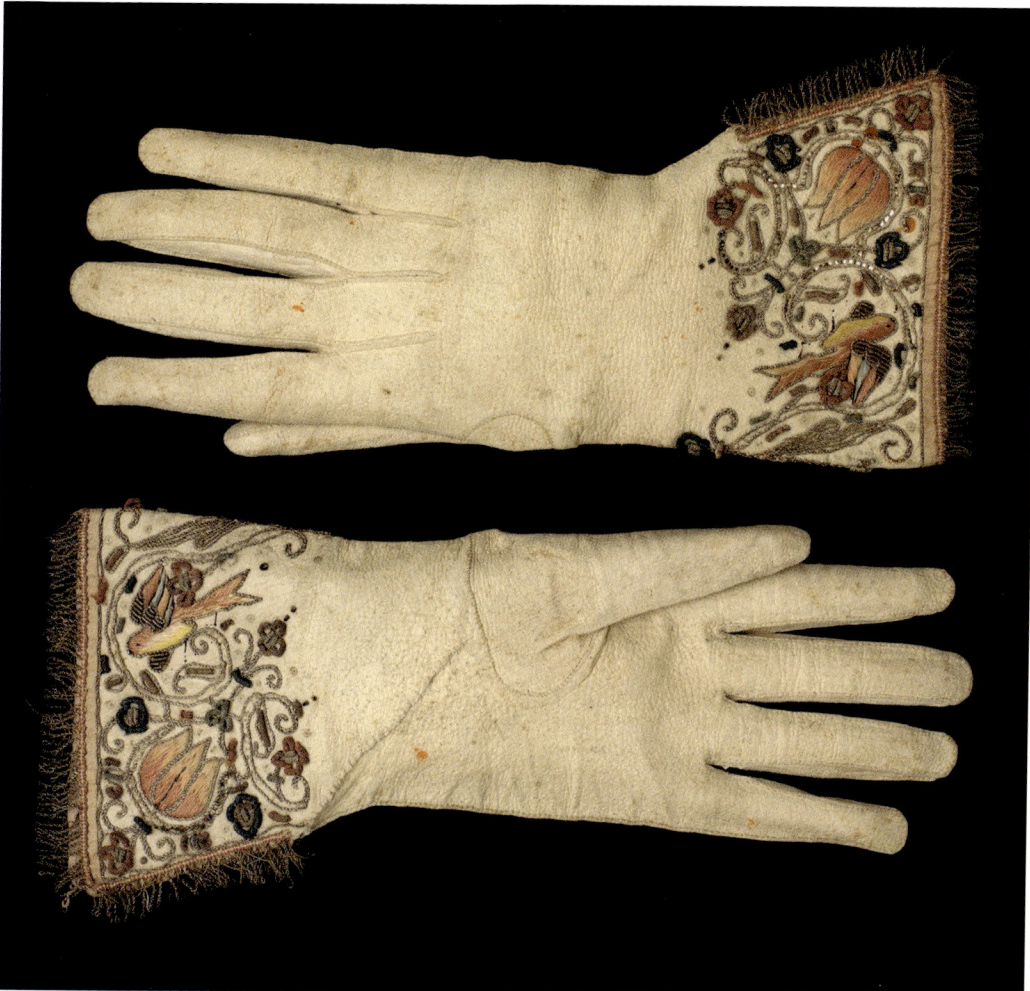

Fig. 80: Gloves, British, about 1630–50 (29.139.a–b)

The embroidery design on the gauntlets of these gloves is worked in coloured silk and silver threads with coiling stems in satin stitch and laid thread work. The metal spangles and silver thread looped fringe braid around the edge of the gauntlet create further embellishment.

That pair are embroidered with an arabesque design that includes a thistle, which may be the only reason for the attribution. Others examples include a single glove in the Spence Collection and a pair in the Lady Lever Art Gallery, purchased by William Hesketh Lever from a private collection at Kilbryde Castle, Perthshire.[9] The closest match is a pair of gloves in the Gallery of Costume, Manchester.[10] The drawing and colours used in the design, in particular the parrot-like birds, and the execution is so similar that both pairs of gloves were probably made in the same workshop.

While the gloves are contemporary with Cromwell, the nightcap dates from the mid to late eighteenth century so certainly never belonged to him. It is embellished with large

pink flowers and smaller blue and yellow buds in crewel wool threads with a blonde lace brim (fig. 82). The pattern is tamboured, a form of embroidery that looks similar to chain stitch, but is made using a tambour needle with a hooked end, rather similar to a fine crotchet hook, that punches through the fabric from the front rather than a needle from the back. The technique originated in India and is not believed to have arrived in Britain until the late 1750s. It is puzzling that Burrell did not question the attribution; even if they did not correctly identify the technique and therefore a terminus first date it is hard to believe that the plain-dressing Puritan Cromwell would have owned such a decorative and 'dainty' floral nightcap.

Fig. 81: Detail of embroidered tulip and bird in fig. 80

Tulips (*Tulipa gesneriana*) were first introduced to Western Europe from the Ottoman Empire (now modern Turkey) in the middle of the sixteenth century. They were particularly popular in the United Provinces (now the Netherlands) where they were seen to be luxury items. The Dutch enthusiasm for the new flowers resulted in tulip mania, with individual bulbs of rare varieties selling for exorbitant prices until the market collapsed in February 1637. Tulips were introduced to England in the late sixteenth century. Whilst they were highly prized and seen as status symbols, the English did not speculate on rare bulbs to the extent that the Dutch did.

Fig. 82: Nightcap, British, about 1770–1800 (29.138)
The colourful embroidery on the nightcap is worked using crewel wool threads. These use long staples, single wool hairs, which are tightly twisted to make fine wool yarns suitable for embroidery.

Restoration Items

The Restoration in 1660 led to an increased interest in fashion radiating out from the lively court of Charles II to the general populace. Glasgow's most recent acquisition of seventeenth-century costume is a small nightcap from this period purchased in 2006 (fig. 83). It is made from six conical sections of richly-coloured red silk velvet heavily embroidered with stylized pomegranates in silver and silver-gilt threads that would have caught the light of the candles at night (fig. 84). The embroidery technique on the nightcap, with its raised and padded work, is found on several items of costume from the mid-seventeenth century, including a pair of mules, about the 1650s–1660s, in the Victoria and Albert Museum, London.[1] It is similar to embroideries worked in the Ottoman Empire and reflects the direct influence of the great trading ventures of the late sixteenth and seventeenth centuries on British taste. English trade with Turkey was well established during the late Tudor period and a treaty between Elizabeth I and Sultan Murad III (1546–95) in 1580 ensured unrestricted trading for the

1 Victoria and Albert Museum, London, T.631&A-1972.

Fig. 83: Nightcap, British, about 1660–80 (29.315)

The main areas of the design are in couched and laid work with each four rows of threads stitched down at regular intervals, staggered with the next four rows to form a basket-weave effect. Highlights are embroidered over thick cords to create a raised and padded design. The edges of the motifs and smaller details are stitched with twisted silver thread. Scattered on the exposed velvet ground are silver spangles sewn on using yellow silk threads. The seams between the six panels that form the nightcap are covered with six-strand plaited silver-gilt braid. The crown is lined with un-dyed linen, cut and shaped in the centre.

Opposite Detail of fig. 85

Fig. 84: Detail of embroidered pomegranate in fig. 83

Pomegranates (*Punica granatum*), which are native to Central Asia, were popular motifs on textiles and clothing from the 1520s through to the late-seventeenth century in the Middle East and Europe. Their name derives from the Latin *pomum* (apple) and *granatus* (seeded), and it is this profusion of seeds that resulted in the pomegranate becoming a general symbol of fertility and a Christian signifier of Jesus' resurrection. The climate in southern Spain suited the cultivation of the fruit and when the joint rulers King Ferdinand of Aragon and Queen Isabella of Castile re-conquered Granada from the Muslims in 1492 they added the pomegranate, the Spanish word for which is *granada*, to their Royal Coat of Arms. The motif became popular in England after their daughter, Catherine of Aragon, married Prince Arthur and later Henry VIII. The pomegranate was subsequently used as a personal device for her daughter, Mary I.

English under their own flag. The following year, the Levant Company was formed, from which the East India Company emerged two decades later in 1600. Trade continued after the Union of the Crowns in 1603 and over the following decades Turkish Bullion embroidery became a prized import and inspired British embroiderers.

The velvet nightcap, dating from the 1660s, is said to have belonged to Major Hugh Buntine (died 1714). A handwritten paper tag attached to the lining of the nightcap states '[t]his cap belonged to Major Buntine, uncle of William Baillie of Monkton. He served under General Lesley in the Civil Wars; and particularly distinguished [sic] at Philiphaugh. Cromwell made him Master of the Horse in Scotland. Monk sent him to Breda to see Charles II'.

Nothing is known about the early life of Hugh Buntine until he joined the Covenanters' army, led by Lieutenant General Sir David Leslie (1601–1682), with whom he fought at the Battle of Philiphaugh on 13 September 1645 and where they enjoyed an outstanding victory over the previously undefeated army of James Graham (1612–50), 1st Marquis of Montrose. As a result of his performance on the field, Oliver Cromwell made Buntine Muster-Master of the Horse in Scotland.[2] He continued to be active during the Commonwealth serving as a Rutmaster, an officer in a cavalry regiment in command of a troop of horse, a rank equivalent to a captain of foot. The Records of the Burgh of Glasgow include letters from Lieutenant-General Robert Montgomery, 12 April 1651, asking the Provost 'to give one rutmaster Buntein ane thowsand merkis'.[3]

Interestingly Buntine must have maintained some sympathy towards the Stuarts, for he was later involved with General George Monck (1608–70) in the Restoration of Charles II. Buntine was hired by Monck in late 1659 to send a letter to Robert Montgomery with a view to using the English army in Scotland to assist with the imposition of a political settlement in England. On 4 April 1660 Charles Stuart made the Declaration of Breda, promising 'liberty to tender consciences', thus smoothing his path back to the thrones of England, Scotland and Ireland. A letter from Sir Robert Moray (1608/9–73) to Alexander Bruce (1629–81), later 2nd Earl of Kincardine, sent from Paris on 23 April 1660, includes the cryptic reference 'I must tell you this Binting is he first wrote to Robert Montegomery to go to 7.

---

2 Robertson (1823), 24–6.
3 Marwick (1881), 197–216.

and then come home 4 moneths ago in his father's name, and I hear Robin is now gone with him to Breda'.[4]

Buntine seems to have prospered in civilian life after the Restoration, earning enough to purchase the Orchard estate, including Law Castle, in Kilbride in 1670. A couple of years later in 1672 an Act of Parliament granted 'in favour of Major Hugh Buntine, his heirs and assignees whatsoever, heritable and irredeemably, of all and whole the lands and barony of Kilbride'.[5] It was during this period that Buntine was appointed one of the Trustees of the Eglinton estate, where he played an instrumental part in the restoration of the fortunes of the estate. The nightcap dates from this peaceful and prosperous period of his life after the Restoration and reflects his new social position as a member of the gentry.

Mid-seventeenth-century nightcaps are shorter with larger diameters than those made in the early 1600s, as they were designed to sit snugly over the crown of the head, rather than perched on top. During 1663 periwigs started to be worn, possibly as a result of Charles II's hair beginning to turn grey. Samuel Pepys first writes of trying one on in his diary for 6 May 1663, although he initially lacked the courage to buy one. He finally ordered his first periwig on 30 October, and describes its arrival on 3 November;

> By and by comes Chapman, the periwigg-maker, and upon my liking it, without more ado I went up, and there he cut off my haire, which went a little to my heart at present to part with it; but, it being over, and my periwigg on, I paid him L3 for it; and away went he with my owne haire to make up another of, and I by and by, after I had caused all my mayds to look upon it; and they conclude it do become me; though Jane was mightily troubled for my parting of my own haire, and so was Besse, I went abroad to the Coffeehouse, … Sir W. Pen observed mightily, and discoursed much upon my cutting off my haire, as he do of every thing that concerns me, but it is over, and so I perceive after a day or two it will be no great matter.

To enable the wigs to fit correctly, gentlemen were required to shave their heads. As a result nightcaps became invaluable accessories, replacing wigs when in private at home.

An object of particular significance is the Burse for the Great Seal (fig. 85). The Great Seal of England is the ultimate symbol of English law, the equivalent to the crown

Opposite **Fig. 85:** Burse of the Great Seal of England, English, about 1682–85 (29.153)

The design of the burses became increasingly standardized during the seventeenth and eighteenth centuries, with the Royal Coat of Arms in the centre with supporters and winged *putti*. In contrast to this splendour, the back of the burse is plain undecorated red velvet. The fastening along the top has drawstring braids in red silk and gilt thread with large tassels at the end that were made from red silk-covered solid shapes with gilt thread over.

4 Moray and Stevenson (2007), 207.
5 Brown (2007).

for the monarchy. It is held by the Keeper of the Great Seal, a role that historically was sometimes combined with the role of Lord High Chancellor and was officially added to that position in 1761. Traditionally a ceremonial purse, known as a 'burse', was made for it annually and was looked after by the wife of the Lord Keeper. When it was replaced the Lord Keeper was allowed to keep the older purse. An invoice from Roger Nelham (died 1654) in 1652 describes 'embroidering the rich purse for the Greate Seale of

Fig. 86: Detail of embroidered Royal Coat of Arms in fig. 85

The Royal Coat of Arms is worked on linen-covered card that is padded with heavy cords and covered with coarse canvas which was possibly stiffened with glue to keep it raised from the surface of the burse. The silver and silver-gilt threads are then laid and couched on top. The arms are mounted like appliqué work on the red silk velvet ground with slip stitches and the edges are covered with silver-gilt wire. The remainder of the ground is further embellished with gilt spangles attached with bullion knots. The burse would have been made by one of Charles II's royal embroiderers, such as William Rutlish (1605–87), who were commissioned to design and make items for the court, including ceremonial objects such as this.

England with best double refined gold and silver upon a rich velvet, ingraine with the arms of the Commonwealth of England at large'.[6] In 1882 the decision was made to stop making new bags annually because of the expense, but to only replace them when they wore out. Several burses for the Great Seal survive, including those belonging to Sir Thomas Egerton (about 1540–1617), Lord Chancellor to Elizabeth I from 1596 to 1603, and another used by Sir Orlando Bridgeman (1606–74), Lord Chancellor to Charles II between 1667 and 1672.[7]

Like many of its kind, the burse is made of red silk velvet embroidered with silver and silver-gilt threads. On the front is the Royal Coat of Arms for Charles II with quartered shield showing the arms of England, Scotland and Ireland, the Crown and supporters (fig. 86). In the top corners are the initials C and R for *Carolus Rex* (King Charles), a rose for England and a thistle for Scotland. At the centre bottom is a depiction of the Orb, which was created for the coronation of Charles II in 1661. There are also four *putti*, winged nude figures in the centre, whilst the wide border is decorated with *putti* heads and cornucopia. The burse would have been made by one of the embroiderers appointed to the court of Charles II. One was William Rutlish (1605–87) who was appointed Court Embroiderer in 1661 and later became Master of the Worshipful Company of Broderers.

The burse was made for Francis North, 1st Baron Guildford, the second son of Dudley North (1602–77), 4th Baron North, and Anne, daughter of Sir Charles Montague (fig. 87). He attended school in Isleworth and Bury St Edmunds before studying at St John's College, Cambridge, in 1653. He left before graduating in order to study law at the Middle Temple in November 1655 and was subsequently called to the bar in June 1661. He married Frances Pope, third daughter of Thomas Pope of Wroxton Abbey on 5 March 1672. They initially settled in Chancery Lane, London, but moved to Wroxton in the 1670s, and in 1681 North bought out the other heirs to the abbey. On 20 December 1682 Charles II appointed him Lord Keeper of the Great Seal, a role he kept until his death in 1685.

The Great Seal contained in these burses was a silver mould in two halves into which softened green or red wax was poured to create the impression of the seal. The wax was

---

6 http://yeomenoftheguard.com/great_seals_of_state.htm
Date accessed: 10 May 2013

7 British Museum, London, M&ME 1997, 1–3, 1 and Weston Park Foundation, Shropshire.

Restoration Items

Fig. 87: Attributed to John Riley, *Francis North, 1st Baron Guildford*, about 1682. Oil on canvas, 127.2 × 103.2 cm. National Portrait Gallery, London

This portrait depicts Francis North in his Lord Keeper's robes with the first of the three burses for the Great Seal that he would have owned prominently displayed on the right.

then hardened in cold water and attached to official documents with strings. In the past it would have been attached to all royal documents, charters, and letters patent so it developed a certain aura due to its importance. Lord Heneage Finch (1621–1682), later 1st Earl of Nottingham, was the predecessor to Francis North and kept the burse under his pillow. When Thomas Sadler broke into his house on 7 February 1677 he was able to steal the mace and burse, but not the Great Seal. Today the Great Seal is only used on a few occasions, such as the election of a new bishop. However, the tradition of having a burse continues. It can be seen carried by the Lord Chancellor at the State Opening of Parliament, but it now contains the Queen's Speech rather than the Great Seal.

Late Seventeenth-century Accessories

Several styles of dress worn during the late sixteenth to the late eighteenth century were variations of an open gown. Often these were cut with their bodices open at the front, leaving a large v-shaped opening that either revealed the front of a pair of decorative stays or, more often, was filled with a triangular panel known as a stomacher that would be pinned, sewn or tied into position each day. Stomachers ranged from plain examples to jewel-encrusted pieces worn at court. An early surviving example (fig. 88) from the late seventeenth century is made from yellow corded silk,

Fig. 88: Stomacher, British, about 1675–1700 (29.147)

The silk embroidery is worked in bullion, satin, split and stem stitches and French knots, whilst the silver thread is laid and couched in place with silk threads with the centre of the rose in basket weave. The silver thread has, with time, oxidized and become black, making the design appear much heavier than originally intended.

Opposite Detail of fig. 90

embroidered with coloured silk and silver threads in a slightly asymmetrical design with a large rose in the centre surrounded by smaller flowers and foliage. The stomacher was acquired by William Burrell in 1910 and for several years hung mounted and framed over the mantelpiece in the Tower Sitting Room at Hutton Castle (see fig. 3).

The latest item of seventeenth-century costume in the collection is a folding fan (fig. 89). Hand-held fans date back several thousand years, with evidence showing that fixed styles were used by the Egyptians and subsequently by the Greeks and Romans. Whilst their use in Europe declined over the subsequent centuries, fans became an important part of Chinese and Japanese culture and led to the development of the folding fan. Elizabeth I is credited with making the fan popular in England; several portraits depict her with white feather examples. It was in the late 1580s that the folding fan was introduced, which was to become the more popular style in Europe. At the newly established court of Louis XIV at Versailles folding fans became an essential female accessory, and led to the foundation in 1673 of the *Association de Eventaillistes* (Association of Fan-makers) in Paris, with Louis as its patron. Fans had decreased in popularity in Britain during the austerity of the

Fig. 89: Fan, Dutch or Italian, about 1690–1700 (1883.32.bf)
The obverse of the leaf depicts King Midas seated in the centre in a blue cloak between the gods Apollo and the goat-legged Pan.

Commonwealth period. However, after the revocation of the Edict of Nantes in 1585 many Protestant Huguenots, including former members of the Association, emigrated to Britain, Holland and Prussia. As a result the last few decades of the seventeenth century saw a flourishing of the fan industry, culminating in the founding of the Worshipful Company of Fan Makers in 1709.

The fan, the oldest example of over 160 fans in the European Costume collection, was made in Holland or Italy in the last decade of the seventeenth century. The sticks and guards are made of ivory, the latter shallowly carved with a figure at the top of each. They are held together at the head with a metal rivet reinforced with a mother-of-pearl washer. The leaf of the fan is created from a single piece of vellum, a thin calf, lamb or kid skin that has been treated to be used as a surface for writing or painting. The front, or obverse, was hand-painted onto the fan leaf before it was mounted to the sticks and guards *à la Anglaise* (in the English style).

The scene depicts the judgement of Midas. Apollo, the Greek and Roman god of the sun and patron god of music and poetry, is shown on the left wearing a yellow cloak playing his lyre, whilst Pan, a lesser god with goat's legs, is on the right playing his pipes or syrinx. Between them in the centre is King Midas, depicted with ass's ears. On either side are Apollo and Pan's respective supporters, with several of the Muses on the left and a nymph and satyrs on the right. The story is from Ovid's *Metamorphoses*,[1] a Roman narrative poem completed in 8 AD. Book 11 tells of King Midas. In a later episode Pan challenges Apollo to a music contest, judged by the mountain god Tmolus, who proclaims Apollo the winner. Midas, a keen follower of Pan, disagrees with the verdict, judging Pan's music to be superior.

The use of a classical scene on the leaf showed the user's education and knowledge, even though by 1690 it was no longer to necessary to know Latin in order to read the *Metamorphoses*. The first English translation, credited to Arthur Golding (about 1536–1605), was published in 1567 and influenced William Shakespeare. A new English translation was published by George Sands in 1626 and subsequently a further seven editions appeared during the course of the seventeenth century.

The reverse of the fan is decorated with a much simpler still-life composition of flowers shown against a dark

---

1 Ovid, *Metamorphoses*, 11:146–193.

background (fig. 90). The selection of flowers includes specimens that were popular during the late seventeenth century. Tulips and carnations were known to be particular favourites of Louis XIV, whilst hyacinths were favoured for their sweet-smelling fragrance. Flowers, that had been immensely popular as embroidered motifs on waistcoats and petticoats in the early 1600s, were slowly beginning to be created on costume using other techniques, such as painted on fans and, increasingly in the eighteenth century, woven into silk cloth.

Fig. 90: Reverse of fan

As the fan leaf is mounted *à la Anglaise*, the back or reverse of the fan was painted directly onto after the leaf had been attached to the ivory sticks and guards and it is just possible to see the outline of the ivory ribs under the layer of paint.

Catalogue Information

Coif (part), British, about 1610–20
Linen with silk and silver-gilt, 21.5cm × 33.5cm
John Hunt; from whom purchased by Sir William Burrell on 24 August for £40. Purchase Book 1937, 33, 'An Elizabethan stomacher of cream linen closely embroidered with a scrolling design of flowers. English, late 16th century. 12" × 9".'
Glasgow Museums, Burrell Collection, 29.17

Coif (part), British, about 1610–20
Linen with silver and silver-gilt, 22cm × 29cm
L. Chamidy; from whom purchased by Sir William Burrell on 30 May for £12. Purchase Book 1925, 9, 'Small panel of Elizabethan embroidery worked in gold & silver thread. 8 inches by 10 inches.'
Glasgow Museums, Burrell Collection, 29.21

Coif, British, about 1610–20
Linen with silk, 23cm × 44.5cm
Frank Partridge and Sons; from whom purchased by Sir William Burrell on 15 February for £115.10. Purchase Book 1946, 17, 'A shaped panel of Elizabethan needlework – a Modesty – finely worked in bright silks with a variety of animals and fabulous beasts and birds among conventional scrolling flowering and fruiting branches.'
Glasgow Museums, Burrell Collection, 29.22

Embroidered panel, British, about 1610–20
Linen with silk and silver-gilt, 20.5cm × 27cm
Glasgow Museums, Burrell Collection, 29.26

Waistcoat, British, about 1600–30 with later alterations
Silk with silver-gilt, centre-back length 44cm
John Hunt; from whom purchased by Sir William Burrell on 24 August for £110. Purchase Book 1937, 31, 'A very unusual Elizabethan woman's jacket or bodice woven of yellow silk and gold thread with a design in beige and gold. The bodice is of typical form with a short flared skirt and the sleeves gathered at the shoulders. The sleeves, which have been woven in one piece, are contracted after the elbow to form a cuff. Length down centre back 16" width across back 9" width across each front 7½". The bodice has been made to pin down the front and was probably not used with a stomacher. Second half of the 16th century.'
Glasgow Museums, Burrell Collection, 29.126

Waistcoat, British, about 1615–18
Linen with silk, silver-gilt, and spangles, centre-back length 47cm
Frank Partridge and Sons; from whom purchased by Sir William Burrell on 15 October for £205. Purchase Book 1930, 22, 'A fine James I Bodice embroidered on cream linen ground with flowers, foliage and fruit in fine needlework.'
Glasgow Museums, Burrell Collection, 29.127

Waistcoat, British, about 1640–60
Silk with linen, centre-back length 83cm

Nightcap, British, about 1640–60
Silk with silver and silver-gilt, silver purl and spangles, 11cm × 19cm × 19cm

Slippers, British, about 1640–60
Silk with silver and silver-gilt, silver purl and spangles, leather, 9cm × 26cm × 11cm
Charles II (possibly); 1645, given to Thomas Veel; by descent; Frank Partridge and Sons; from whom purchased by Sir William Burrell on 6 August for £125. Purchase Book 1937, 36–37, 'A cap, tunic and shoes worn by Charles II when as Prince of Wales in 1645 he was sent to take charge of the Royalist forces in the West of England. The cap is of salmon pink richly embroidered with silver bullion. The shoes of similar colour made to match. The tunic is of silk quilted throughout (on this occasion Charles stayed in the house of Colonel Thomas Veel of Alverstone near Bristol and left these things as a souvenir of his visit. They have been handed down in the family & have recently been purchased from a direct descendant).'
Glasgow Museums, Burrell Collection, 29.128, 29.133 and 29.144–145

Coif, British, about 1610–15
Linen with silver, silver-gilt and silver bobbin lace, 22.5cm × 43cm
Glasgow Museums, Burrell Collection, 29.130

Coif, British, about 1610–20
Linen with silk and silver gilt spangles, 24cm × 43.5cm
John Hunt; from whom purchased by Sir William Burrell on 8 September for £18. Purchase Book 1938, 45, 'A small Elizabethan cap-piece finely embroidered on linen – Embroidery, floral designs in beads with gilt metal sequins between the embroidered rows.'
Glasgow Museums, Burrell Collection, 29.131

Nightcap, British, about 1600–20
Linen with silk and silver-gilt, 20cm × 18cm × 18cm
Major W. G. Townsend Currie; Frank Partridge and Sons; from whom purchased by Sir William Burrell on 22 January for £18. Purchase Book 1943, 41, 'A linen cap embroidered with acorns in black silk and with scroll work in gold thread. Elizabethan. From the Collection of Major Currie, Christleton, near Chester.'
Glasgow Museums, Burrell Collection, 29.132

Coif and forehead cloth, British, about 1610–20
Linen with silk and silver, 24cm × 41cm; 16cm × 35cm
Frank Partridge and Sons; from whom purchased by Sir William Burrell on 24 September for £75. Purchase Book 1936, 61, 'Rare Elizabethan Lady's Cap finely embroidered with silks in various colours with birds & leaves & scroll work in gilt thread & sequins, all embroidered on fine linen.'
Glasgow Museums, Burrell Collection, 29.134

Nightcap, British, about 1600–20
Linen with silk and silver-gilt, spangles and bobbin lace, 18cm × 18cm × 18cm
Frank Partridge and Sons; from whom purchased by Sir William Burrell on October 22 for £75. Purchase Book 1937, 58, 'An Elizabethan needlework cap with a design of flowers in natural colours on a cream ground.'
Glasgow Museums, Burrell Collection, 29.135

Nightcap, British, about 1600–20
Linen with silk and silver-gilt, 20cm × 18cm × 18cm (if complete)
Royal School of Needlework; from whom purchased with two other panels by William Burrell on 31 December for £116. Purchase Book 1925, 30, '3 Elizabethan panels.'
Glasgow Museums, Burrell Collection, 29.136

Panel of blackwork, British, about 1600–20
Linen with silk, 23cm × 31cm
Glasgow Museums, Burrell Collection, 29.137

Nightcap, British, about 1770–1800
Linen with wool and bobbin lace, 12cm × 19cm × 19cm

Gloves, British, circa 1630–1650
Leather with silk and silver-gilt thread, 14cm × 31cm
John Hunt; from whom purchased by Sir William Burrell on 30 September for £65. Purchase Book 1937, 49, 'A cap, gloves & two combs formerly the property of Oliver Cromwell in a leather case, together with two letters proving their authenticity. The cap is linen embroidered in brilliant colours with a fine lace border. The gloves embroidered in bullion work, in brilliant colours & metal thread. The combs are tortoiseshell, one finely engraved' and newspaper cutting 'These dainty __ Noll left behind him at Chard when he retreated before the advancing army of Charles I in July, 1645 .... They were placed in a Chard church vault, where they stayed until two years ago, when the owner of the vault gave them away to settle a debt.'
Glasgow Museums, Burrell Collection, 29.138 and 29.139

Gloves, British, about 1610–30
Leather with silk and silver-gilt, 21cm × 32cm
Lord Grantley; Frank Partridge and Sons; from whom purchased by Sir William Burrell on 27 August for £26. Purchase Book 1942, 26, 'A pair of Stuart gloves of buff coloured leather, the gauntlets of cream satin embroidered in coloured silks and gold thread with formal flower branches, the ground sewn with sequins, the borders outlined with narrow gold lace with pendant sequins. Lord Grantley sale.'
Glasgow Museums, Burrell Collection, 29.141.1–2

Stomacher, English, about 1675–1700
Silk with silk and silver, 40cm × 29cm
Jan A Lewis & Son; from whom purchased by Sir William Burrell on 15 May for £10. Purchase Book 1919, 16, 'Stuart embroidered needle work stomacher.'
Glasgow Museums, Burrell Collection, 29.147

Handkerchief, British, about 1600–25
Linen with silk and silver, 38cm × 37cm
John Hunt; from whom purchased by Sir William Burrell on 1 September for £22. Purchase Book 1939, 39, 'An English Elizabeth handkerchief of linen, the bordered finely embroidered with conventional designs in "black work" and gold with initials in one corner. Illustrated in Seligman's book "Domestic Needlework" plate 35A, Size 15 × 14".
Glasgow Museums, Burrell Collection, 29.148

Falconry pouch, British, early seventeenth century
Leather with silk, silver, silver-gilt, gold, glass and wood, 36cm × 46cm × 6cm

Falconry glove, British, early seventeenth century
Leather with silk, silver, silver-gilt and wood, 180cm × 390cm

Lure, British, early seventeenth century
Wood, linen, feathers, silk, silver, silver-gilt, 20cm × 14cm × 5cm

Hood, British, early seventeenth century
Leather, wool, linen, brass, feather, 8cm × 11cm × 6cm

Hood, British, early seventeenth century
Leather, wool, linen, brass, feather, and feather, 9cm × 7cm × 6cm
James VI and I (1566–1625); 1619, Sir William Pope (1573–1631), 1st Earl of Downe; by descent; Percival Griffiths; 1932, purchased by Frank Partridge & Sons from Percival Griffiths for £1,050; from whom purchased by Sir William Burrell 1934 for £1,100. Purchase Book 1934, 19–20, 'A set of Falconers Accoutrements, early 17th Century, comprising a bag 17" wide in leather, decorated in gold and silver, couched in coloured silks, the whole with gold fringe and a graceful gold mount decorated with brilliant enamel with two branches of bramble bearing leaving, flowers and fruit. Bramble and mistletoe form main decorative motif in embroidery which also appears on the gauntlet glove and the lure enhanced by much gold decoration. From the embroidered [illegible] in the panel hang the tessellated cords from which falcon [illegible] were hung. The limbs of the lure are of wonderful workmanship clothed in a series of horizontal rings of goldwork, there are also two hoods. The set as a whole is a wonderful example of Jacobean Art, while the Elizabethan influence was still being felt. The gold and enamel work was the work of George Heriot. This was left at Wroxton near Banbury by King James I as a souvenir of his visit to Lord Dudley North. From the collection of Percival Griffiths FSA Sandridgebury, near St Albans. Illustrated in Domestic Needlework by Seligman & Hughes, Plate 57'.
Glasgow Museums, Burrell Collection, 29.151.1–5

Hood, British, before 1603
Leather, silk and silver-gilt, 9cm × 7cm × 6cm
John Hunt; from whom purchased by Sir William Burrell on 20 December for £28. Purchase Book 1938, 80, 'An usually important hawks-hood of leather and velvet, embroidered with gold gallon, the leather stamped with a design, the top ornamented with a tuft.

Late 16th or early 17th century. The hood is much larger than was usual and was evidently made for an important person. Only the very highest nobility were allowed to use very big hawks and this hood was made for a big falcon. Height 2¼" × 2½".'
Glasgow Museums, Burrell Collection, 29.151.6

Falconry glove, southern Germany, late seventeenth century
Leather, silk and silver-gilt, 14cm × 36cm

Hood, southern Germany, late seventeenth century
Leather, silk and silver-gilt, 13cm × 13cm × 7cm

Bag, southern Germany, late sixteenth–seventeenth century
Leather, silk, 18cm × 12cm × 12cm

Hunting accessory, southern Germany, late seventeenth century
Leather, linen, metal, 40cm × 14cm × 5cm
Purchased by Sir William Burrell from Sothebys, London, via Acton Surgey on 11 December 1931 for £65. Purchase Book 1932, 48, 'A finely embroidered hawking set.'
Glasgow Museums, Burrell Collection, 29.152.1–4

Burse of the Great Seal of England, English, about 1682–85
Silk with silver and silver-gilt, purls and spangles, 43cm × 40.5cm
1682–5, Sir Francis North (1637–85), 1st Baron Guildford; by descent; 1933, presumed sold in the Wroxton Abbey sale 22–29 May; 1948, purchased by Sir William Burrell from Acton Surgey on 22 June for £170. Purchase Book 1948, 79, 'A Royal coat of Arms of superlative quality in the form of a Chancellor's purse. The stumpwork features are raised in heavy relief with the Crown and Royal arms, perforated similar to undercut wood work. The appliqué work is mostly white and yellow gold on an old red velvet ground. The initials CR connected to the Royal rose and Scottish thistle must relate to Charles II as understand the purse belonged to Francis North who became Baron Guildford and retained the Chancellors Seal until his death in 1685. The purse was sold by the North Settled Estates Heirlooms. Size of purse excluding the tassels and cords
1 ft 4" wide × 1 ft 5" high. Size includes of tassels and cords 33¾ × 23½.'
Glasgow Museums, Burrell Collection, 29.153

Bag, British, late seventeenth century
Silk with silk, 18cm × 24cm × 24cm
Debenham and Freebody; from whom purchased by Sir William Burrell on 17 July for £8. Purchase Book 1917, 26, 'Stuart needlework bag.'
Glasgow Museums, Burrell Collection, 29.154

Sweet bag, British, about 1600–30
Silk with silk, silver and silver-gilt thread, wood 14cm × 14.5cm
John Hunt; from whom purchased by Sir William Burrell on 27 June for £12. Purchase Book 1938, 22, 'A small needlework purse of very brilliant colouring covered in flowers etc on a silver ground 4¾ × 5½".'
Glasgow Museums, Burrell Collection, 29.155

Coif, British, about 1610–20
Linen with silver and silver-gilt, silver spangles and bobbin lace, 45cm × 26.5cm
Glasgow Museums, Burrell Collection, 29.294.a

Sweet bag, British, about 1600–30
Silk with silk, silver and silver-gilt thread, 33cm × 17cm
1989, purchased by Bernheimer Fine Arts Limited; 1991, purchased from Bernheimer Fine Arts Limited for £16,500 by the Trustees of the Burrell Collection.
Glasgow Museums, Burrell Collection, 29.310

Petticoat, British, about 1610–20
Silk with silk and silver, 91cm × 313cm
Anne of Denmark (possibly); by descent to Charles I (possibly); acquired by William Levett; by descent to Catherine Levett, wife of Rev Edward Dering; by descent to John Thurlow Dering; about 1820 Anne Dering marries William Lee Warner olim Bagge; by descent through the Lee Warner family to Mrs Bulwer-Long; purchased from Christie's, South Kensington, London, sale no.TEX-7407 'Important Costume, Needlework and Textile Designs, including the J. S. Wheelwright Archive' on 19 November 1996 for £52,050 by the Burrell Trustees with the assistance of The Art Fund.
Glasgow Museums, Burrell Collection, 29.314

Nightcap, about 1660–80
Silk with silver and silver-gilt, 15cm × 20cm × 20cm
Purchased from Christies, St James, London, sale no.7306 'Out of the Ordinary: The discerning and individual taste of Christopher Gibbs and Harris Lindsay' on 10 May 2006 for £2,200, by the Burrell Trustees with the assistance of The Art Fund.
Glasgow Museums, Burrell Collection, 29.315

Fan, Dutch or Italian, about 1690–1700
Oil on vellum mounted on ivory, 27.2cm × 46.2cm
Museum purchase.
Glasgow Museums, 1883.32.bf

***Reticella* with *dentate punto in aria* edging, Venetian, late 16th-early 17th century**
Linen, 18cm × 9cm
Museum Purchase.
Glasgow Museums, 1888.19.k

Gloves, British, about 1610–30
Leather with silk and silver-gilt, 14.5cm × 31cm
Museum Purchase from Christie's, South Kensington, London, 1977.
Glasgow Museums, E.1977.111.a–b

Biographies of Collectors and Dealers

Sir William Burrell (1861–1958)
The third son of William Burrell (1832–85), a shipping owner, and his wife, Isabella Duncan Guthrie (died 1912). He was educated at boarding-school at St Andrews before joining Burrell & Son, a Glaswegian shipping firm founded by his grandfather, George Burrell. He later became co-manager with his eldest brother. In 1917 he sold his interest in the firm and dedicated his time to collecting tapestries, paintings, stained glass, sculpture, ceramics, armour, embroideries and Islamic rugs. Burrell gifted his collection to Glasgow in 1944 and continued to add pieces until his death.

Major W. G. Townsend Currie (b. 1879)
The only surviving son of Captain Richard Henry Williams Currie (1833–89) of Boughton Hall, Cheshire, and his wife, Charlotte Graham (died 1908). He served in the British Army, and was active in the invasion of Tibet in 1904. He married Mabel Frances Parnall in 1908. The couple lived at Christleton Old Hall, Cheshire. His paintings collection was sold at Christie, Manson and Wood, London, on 3 June 1932.

John Richard Brinsley Norton, 5th Baron Grantley (1855–1943)
The son of Thomas Norton (1831–77), 4th Baron Grantley, and his wife Maria Federigo. He was educated at Harrow School and Dresden University. He married Katharine Buckner Norton, née McVickar (died 1897), the ex-wife of his cousin, Charles Grantley Campbell Norton, in 1879. He subsequently married Alice Jones (died 1942), daughter of Thomas Heron Jones, 7th Viscount Ranelagh. Norton was a major collector of coins, becoming a Fellow of the Society of Antiquaries of London, the Royal Numismatic Society and the British Numismatic Society. After his death, the coin collection was sold in a series of 11 sales by Glendining in 1943–45.

Percival Griffiths (about 1862–1937)
A London-based chartered accountant in the firm of Deloitte, Plender, Griffiths, and Company. He was an avid collector of English furniture of 1660–1760, but also collected seventeenth-century English domestic embroideries. He purchased Sandridgebury, near St Albans, Hertfordshire, in about 1900, which he used to showcase his collections. His embroidery collection was the subject of a four-part article by Eugenie Gibson in *The Connoisseur*, 1921–22. Between 1927 and 1937 Griffiths kept account books with annotated images of his needlework and silver collections. Griffiths sold part of his collection through the dealer Frank Partridge in 1929, including 22 pieces that were acquired by the Metropolitan Museum of Art, New York. After his death, as a result of a fox-hunting accident, his widow, Gertrude, and the executors of his estate sold most of his collections in a series of sales.

John Hunt (1900–1976)
Studied medicine and architecture before becoming an antique dealer with premises in Bury Street, London. He met his future wife, Gertrude Hartman, who was also interested in fine and decorative art, in the early 1930s. During that decade the Hunts acquired items on behalf not only of Sir William Burrell, but also the American collector, William Randolph Hearst. The Hunts' own collection is now at the Hunt Museum in Limerick, Ireland.

Frank Partridge (1875–1953)
The son of Robert Partridge, who owned a book-making business in Hertfordshire, and his wife Eliza. He founded the art dealers Partridges in 1900, with premises at 26 King Street, London and 741 Fifth Avenue, New York.
The firm, which later traded as **Frank Partridge & Son**, acted as agents for several needlework collectors, including Sir William Burrell and Irwin Untermyer, the latter of whom they became sole agents for. In 1944 the London office moved as a result of the Blitz to premises at 144–146 New Bond Street, London.

Sir Frederick Richmond (1873–1953)
Initially employed as an apprentice at the London department store, Debenham and Freebody, Richmond worked his way up and succeeded Ernest Debenham to become Chairman in 1927. In 1929 he was created a Baronet. He started collecting needlework in about 1907 and during his tenure at Debenham and Freebody he founded a department specializing in selling antique needlework. His private collection was displayed in his town house, 10 Kensington Palace Gardens, London, and at his country house, Westoning Manor, Bedfordshire, purchased after 1936. There were two articles published on the collection by A. F. Kendrick in *The Connoisseur*, in 1935. After his death a selection of items was bequeathed to the Victoria and Albert Museum, London, whilst the remainder of his collection was inherited by his two children. Parts of his collection were subsequently sold at Christie's, South Kensington, London, in 2001 and at Bonhams, London, in 2011.

Glossary

Blackwork
A type of embroidery worked in black silk on linen.

Bobbin lace
Lace made on a pillow with the design laid out in pins and worked with threads attached to bobbins. The threads are woven, plaited or twisted to form an openwork pattern.

Coif
A small linen under-cap with a curved shape around the face to the ears. Often embroidered and sometimes worn with a matching forehead cloth.

Cutwork
A needle lace made by cutting out squares of fabric and then filling the spaces with geometric designs in thread.

Doublet
A jacket with fitted body, skirts, and full-length sleeves.

Ell
A historic measurement based on the length of a man's arm. The exact length varied between countries from approximately 37 inches (94cm) fingertip to shoulder in Scotland, 45 inches (114cm) fingertip to opposite shoulder in England and 54 inches (137cm) fingertip to opposite elbow in France.

Farthingale
A petticoat with hoops of wood, cane or whalebone used to expand the width of the skirt.

Forehead cloth
A triangular piece of linen worn with the long edge over the forehead tied with two long ties and the point behind. Often embroidered and worn with a matching coif.

Forepart
A decorative panel on an under-petticoat, worn to infill an open gown or petticoat.

Gauntlet
An extended cuff on a glove that extends over the wrist.

Needlelace
A lace made using a continuous thread and needle, generally worked on parchment.

Nightcap
A man's cap in linen. Originally worn at night, but later embroidered versions were worn as informal *déshabillé* or undress wear.

Passing
A metal thread with a thin strip of silver or silver-gilt wrapped around a silk core.

Petticoat
A skirt or under-skirt.

Purl
A coil of metal wire.

Silver-gilt
A metal thread made with a thin layer of gold on a silver base.

Spangle
A small thin disk of metal used as a decoration.

Stomacher
A decorative v-shaped panel to infill an open bodice or gown.

Vest
A man's coat with body cut in one with the skirts and full-length sleeves.

Waistcoat
An informal jacket.

GLOSSARY OF STITCHES

Chain stitch
A linked, loop stitch that when repeated forms a chain.

Cross stitch
A double stitch in the shape of a diagonal cross. Also known as gros point when worked on canvas.

Couching
Stitching one thread, often metal, onto a cloth using another, finer thread.

Cutwork
Needlework with parts of the fabric cut away to form a pattern, and either in-filled with needle lace or edges embroidered around.

Detached buttonhole stitch
A loop stitch detached from the fabric using the row above as its ground.

Plaited braid stitch
An interlocked stitch imitating a braid.

Stem stitch
A stitch with very slight diagonal overlap.

Bibliography

BOOKS AND ARTICLES

Abegg, M. 1978. *Apropos Patterns: For embroidery, lace and woven textiles*, Riggisberg, Abagg-Stiftung

Arnold, J. 1980. Jane Lambarde's Mantle, *Costume* 14, 56–72

Arnold, J. 1985. *Patterns of Fashion: The cut and construction of clothes for men and women c1560–1620*, London, Macmillan London Ltd

Arnold, J. 1988. *Queen Elizabeth's Wardrobe Unlock'd*, London, W. S. Maney & Son

Arnold, J. 2000. 'Serpents and Flowers: Embroidery Designs from Thomas Trevelyon's Miscellanies of 1608 and 1616' in *Costume* 34, 7–12

Arnold, J. 2008. *Patterns of Fashion 4: The cut and construction of linen shirts, smocks, neckwear, headwear and accessories for men and women c1540–1660*. London, Macmillan London Ltd

Arthur, L. 1995. *Embroidery 1600–1700 at the Burrell Collection*, London, John Murray in association with Glasgow Museums

Arthur, L. 1995. Seventeenth-century embroideries in the Burrell Collection, *The Magazine Antiques*, June, 854–863

Ashelford, J. 1988. *Dress in the Age of Elizabeth I*, London, B. T. Batsford

Bacon, F. 1625. Of Masques and Triumphs, *Essayes or Counsels, Civill and Morall*, London

Borkopp-Restle, B. 2002. *Textile Schätze aus Renaissance und Barock*, Munich, Bayerisches-National Museum

Brooke, X. 1992. *The Lady Lever Art Gallery Catalogue of Embroideries*, Stroud, Alan Sutton in association with National Museums and Galleries on Merseyside

Brooks, M. M. 2004. *English Embroideries of the Sixteenth and Seventeenth Centuries in the collection of the Ashmolean Museum*, London, Jonathan Horne Publications in association with the Ashmolean Museum

Brown, K. M. et al (eds) 2007. *The Records of the Parliaments of Scotland to 1707*, St Andrews, University of St Andrews

Buck, A. 2000. 'Clothing and textiles in Bedfordshire inventories 1617–1620' in *Costume* 34, 25–38

Busino, O. 1618, *Anglipotrida*

Buss, C. (ed) 2009. *Silk Gold Crimson: Secrets and Technology at the Visconti and Sforza Courts*, Milan, Silvana

Byrde, P. and Brears, P. 1990. 'A pair of James I's gloves', *Costume* 24, 34–42

Capwell, T. 2007. *The Real Fighting Stuff: Arms and Armour at Glasgow Museums*, Glasgow, Glasgow Museums Publishing

Carey, J. 2009. *Sweet Bags: An Investigation into 16th and 17th Century Needlework*, Ottery St Mary: Carey Company

Linthicum, M. C. 1936. *Costume in the Drama of Shakespeare and his Contemporaries*, Oxford, Oxford University Press

Chapman, G. 1606. *Sir Gyles Goosecape*, London

Clifford, D. J. H. (ed) 1992. *The Diaries of Lady Anne Clifford, 1590–1676*, Stroud, Alan Sutton

Cumming, V. 1982. *Gloves*, London, B. T. Batsford Ltd

Cumming, V. 1984. *A Visual History of Costume: The Seventeenth Century*, London, B. T. Batsford Ltd

Cunnington, C. W. and Cunnington, P. 1955. *Handbook of English Costume in the Seventeenth Century*, London, Faber and Faber

Cunnington, P. and Mansfield A. 1969. *English Costume for Sports and Outdoor Recreation*, London, Adam & Charles Black

Digby, G. 1963. *Elizabethan Embroidery*, London, Faber & Faber

Foster, V. 1982. *Bags and Purses*, London, B. T. Batsford Ltd

Foster, V. 1980. "'A Garden of Flowers' A note on some unusual embroidered gloves" in *Costume* 14, 91–94

Fraser, A. 1984. *The Weaker Vessel*, London, Weidenfeld

Gostelow, M. 1976. *Blackwork*, London, B. T. Batsford Ltd

Hackenbroch, Y. 1960. *English and Other Needlework, Tapestries and Textiles in the Irwin Untermyer Collection*, London Thames & Hudson

Hart, A. and North, S. 1998. *Historical Fashion in Detail: The 17th and 18th Centuries*, London, Victoria and Albert Museum Publications

Hogarth, S. 1989. 'The Stapleton-Wyvill marriage purse' in *Textile History* 20(1), 21–32

Howey, C. L. 2007. Dissertation on Busy Bodies: Women, Power and Politics at the Court of Elizabeth I, 1558–1603, New Jersey, New Brunswick

Hurry, J. 1930. *The Woad Plant and Its Dye*, London, Oxford University Press

Jones, A. R. and Stallybrass, P. 2000. *Renaissance Clothing and the Materials of Memory*, Cambridge, Cambridge University Press

King, D. and Levey, S. 1993. *The Victoria and Albert Museum's Textile Collection. Embroidery in Britain from 1200 to 1750*, London, Victoria and Albert Museum Publications

Lawson, W. 1631. *The Country Housewife's Garden*, London

McClure, N. E. (ed) 1939. *The Letters of John Chamberlain*, Philadelphia, Philadelphia, The American Philosophical Society

Mactaggart, P. and Mactaggart, M. 1980. 'The Rich Wearing Apparel of Richard, 3rd Earl of Dorset' in *Costume* 14, 41–55

Marwick, J. D. 1881. *Extracts from the Records of the Burgh of Glasgow vol. 2: 1630–1662*, 197–216 http://www.british-history.ac.uk/report.aspx?compid=47740. Date accessed: 10 May 2013

Moray, R. and Stevenson, D. 2007. *Letters of Sir Robert Moray to the Earl of Kincardine, 1657–73*, Aldershot, Ashgate

Morrall, A. and Watt, M. 2008. *English Embroidery from The Metropolitan Museum of Art, 1580–1700; 'Twixt Nature and Art*, New York, New Haven and London, Yale University Press

Morrill, J. 2004. 'Cromwell, Oliver (1599–1658)'. *Oxford Dictionary of National Biography*, Oxford, Oxford University Press http://www.oxforddnb.com/view/article/6765, accessed 10 May 2013

Morrison, F. 1617. *An Itinerary: Containing His Ten Yeeres Travell through the Twelve Dominions of Germany, Bohmerland, Sweitzerland, Netherland, Denmarke, Poland, Italy, Turky, France, England, Scotland & Ireland*, Volume 4, reprinted Glasgow, James MacLehose and Sons

Nichols, J. 1828. *The Progresses, Processions, and Magnificent Festivities of King James the First, His Royal Consort, Family and Court*, 4 volumes, London

North, S. and Tiramani, J. (eds) 2011. *Seventeenth-Century Women's Dress Patterns: Book 1*, London, V&A Publishing

Paterson, J. 1852. *History of the County of Ayr. Vol. II*, Edinburgh, Thomas George Stevenson

Paterson, J. 1863. *History of the Counties of Ayr and Wigton*, Edinburgh, James Stillie

Payne, M. T. W. 2001. 'An Inventory of Queen Anne of Denmark's 'ornaments, furniture, householde stuffe, and other parcels' at Denmark House', *Journal of the History of Collections* 13 (1), 23–44

Pepys, S. 1661. *Diary*. Latham, R. C. and Matthews, W. (ed) 2000. California, Harper Collins

Pepys, S. 1663. *Diary*. Latham, R. C. and Matthews, W. (ed) 2000. California, Harper Collins

Pepys, S. 1666. *Diary*. Latham, R. C. and Matthews, W. (ed) 2000. California, Harper Collins

Perrin, E. G. 1918, *The Autobiography of Phineas Pett*, London, Navy Records Society

Pope-Hennessy, J. (ed) 1995. *The Life of Benvenuto Cellini, Written by Himself*. Translated by John Addison Symonds, London, Phaidon Press

Pulliam, D. 2002. 'Knitted Silk and Silver: those mysterious jackets'. *Silk Roads, Other Roads: Textile Society of America 8th Biennial Symposium*, Northampton, Massachusetts, Smith College, 173–177

Riberio, A. 1979. "A Paradise of Flowers': Flowers in English Dress in the late sixteenth and early seventeenth centuries', *The Connoisseur* June, 110–117

Riberio, A. 2000. *The Gallery of Fashion*, London, National Portrait Gallery

Riberio, A. 2005. *Fashion and Fiction: Dress in Art and Literature in Stuart England*, New Haven and London, Yale University Press

Robertson, G. 1823. *A Genealogical Account of the Principal Families in Ayrshire*, Irvine, Cunninghame Press

Rothstein, N. (ed) 1984. *Four Hundred Years of Fashion*, London, Victoria and Albert Museum Publications

Rutt, R. 1987. *A History of Hand Knitting*, London, B. T. Batsford Ltd

Seaward, S. 2004. 'Charles II (1630–1685)'. *Oxford Dictionary of National Biography*, Oxford, Oxford University Press, http://www.oxforddnb.com/view/article/5144, accessed 10 May 2013

Shakespeare, W. 1597. *Henry IV, Part 2*, London

Shakespeare, W. about 1595–6. *A Midsummer Night's Dream*, London

Shakespeare, W. about 1599–1601. *Hamlet*, London

Shirley, E. 1869. 'An inventory of the effects of Henry Howard K G Earl of Northampton taken on his death in 1614. Together with a transcript of his will', *Archaeologia* 42, 347–378

Shorleyker, R. 1624. *A Schole-house for the Needle*, London

Steen, S. J. (ed) 1994. *The Letters of Lady Arbella Stuart*, Oxford, Oxford University Press

Swain, M. 1973. *The Needlework of Mary, Queen of Scots*, New York and London, Van Nastrand Reinhold Company

Symonds, R. W. 1931. 'Sandridgebury, the country residence of Percival D Griffiths', *Antiques*, 193–6

Synge, L. 1982. *Antique Embroidery*, London, Blandford Press

Tarrant, N. 1994. *The Development of Costume*, London and Edinburgh, Routledge in association with National Museums of Scotland

Turner, W. 1551, *A Newe Herball*, London

Vincent, S. 1999. 'To Fashion a Self: Dressing in Seventeenth-Century England' in *Fashion Theory*, 3(2), 197–218

Vincent, S. 2003. *Dressing the Elite*, Oxford & New York, Berg

Wardle, P. 1994. 'The King's Embroiderer: Edmund Harrison (1590–1667): I. The Man and his Milieu', *Textile History*, 25 (1), 29–59

Wardle, P. 1995. 'The King's Embroiderer: Edmund Harrison (1590–1667): II. His Work', *Textile History*, 26(2), 139–184

Wardle, P. 2001. 'John Shepley (1575–1631), Embroiderer to the High and Mighty Prince Charles, Prince of Wales', *Textile History*, 32(2), 133–155

Warmington, A. 2004. 'Veel, Thomas (c.1591–1663/4)', *Oxford Dictionary of National Biography*, Oxford, Oxford, University Press http://www.oxforddnb.com/view/article/28171, accessed 10 May 2013

Wilcox, C. 1999. *Bags*, London, Victoria and Albert Museum Publications

Bodleian Library, Papers of the Freke Family of Hannington, Wiltshire, MSS. Eng. misc. c.201–3, c.338–9. Personal accounts of William Freke at Oxford and the Middle Temple, 1619–39

Illustrated London News, 1936, volume 189, no.5085, 533

Index

Anne of Denmark 17, 19, 25, 57, 63, 67, 71, 72, 73, 87, 97
Aragon, Catherine of 51
Aragon, King Ferdinand of 124
Arnold, Janet 67, 68
Association de Eventaillistes 134

Bacon, Francis 49
bags 86, 94, 95, 97–103
Bath Fashion Museum 60, 61, 118
Batten, Martha 80
Battle of Edgehill 111
Battle of Langport 111, 118
Battle of Naseby 118
Battle of Philiphaugh 125
Bayerisches-National Museum 93, 94
Berkeley Castle 117
Berwick upon Tweed 11
Bessemer, Sir Henry 75
blackwork 32–34, 49, 51–55
bobbin lace 79
Bowes Museum 11
Braganza, Catherine of 23, 25
brick stitch 101, 102
Bridgeman, Sir Orlando 129
British Museum 102
Broderers Company 17, 129
Browne, Sir Hugh 62
bullion knot stitch 38, 80, 129, 133
Buntine, Major Hugh 125, 126
burden stitch 84, 85
Burrell Collection 7, 10, 11, 60, 109
Burrell, Lady Constance 11
Burrell, Sir William 10, 11, 13, 42, 47, 93, 108, 111, 118, 134
burse 126, 129–131
Busino, Orazio 27
buttonhole stitch 29, 33, 38, 39, 41, 45, 48, 58, 63, 101, 141

Calvinists 25
Cambridge University 80
Capel, Arthur 19, 111
Capel, Lady Elizabeth 19
Capel Family 19
Carisbrooke Castle 71
Carleton, Dudley 75
Cary, Lady Dorothy 62, 65

Castile, Queen Isabella of 124
Castle Hedingham 93
Catherine of Aragon 51
Catherine of Braganza 23, 25
Cellini, Benvenuto 30
Ceylon stitch 33, 45
chain stitch 29, 33, 44–47, 52, 58, 120, 141
Chamberlain, John 75
Charles I 10, 13, 17, 19, 28, 71, 72, 77
Charles II 5, 6, 13, 17, 21, 23, 25, 111–121, 123, 125, 126, 129
Charles IX 68
Chatham 29
Civil War 13, 19, 25, 111, 117, 125
Clifford, Lady Anne 68, 75
coif 12, 13, 27, 30, 31, 37–49, 53, 55
Columbus, Christopher 113
Commonwealth 19, 25, 118, 125, 129, 135
Company of Broderers 17, 129
Company of Fan Makers 135
Company of Glovers 77
Corbet, Sir John 21, 22
couching 47, 54, 70, 71, 81, 84, 113, 123, 129, 133, 141
Cromwell, Oliver 13, 25, 111–121, 125
cross stitch 35, 38, 51, 52, 141
Currie, Major 35
cushions 10, 13, 46, 47, 98
cutwork 17, 41, 63

Danckerts, Hendrick 23
de Critz the Elder, John 17, 19
Degas, Edgar 12
Denmark House 57, 73, 97
Denmark, Anne of 17, 19, 25, 57, 63, 67, 71, 72, 73, 87, 97
Dering, John Thurlow 71
Dering, Reverend Edward 71
Dering, William 71
déshabillé 27, 35, 105, 114
Devereux, Robert 102
Dobson, William 112
doublet 19, 21, 62, 78, 112, 114

East India Company 15, 125

East Indies 15, 25
Edgehill, Battle of 111
Edict of Nantes 21, 25, 135
Edinburgh 15, 17, 87
Edward VI 15
Egerton, Sir Thomas 129
Elector Palatine 75
Elizabeth I 15, 25, 30, 37, 41, 57, 62, 67, 68, 72, 80, 93, 105, 123, 129, 134
Elizabeth of York 60
ell 67
English Heritage 17, 65, 69, 74, 78

faggot stitch 54, 55
Fairfax, General Thomas 111
falconry accessories 12, 83–95
fan 9, 134, 135, 136, 139
Fashion Museum, Bath 60, 61, 118
Feilding, William 116, 117
Ferdinand, King of Aragon 124
Folger Shakespeare Library 32
forehead cloth 41–43
forepart 69
Fouquet, Jean 62
Frank Partridge & Son 13
Frederick V 75
Freke, William 32
French farthingales 72, 73

Gallery of Costume, Manchester 99, 119
gauntlet 77, 84, 95, 118–119
Gheeraerts, Marcus 33, 51, 52, 63
Glasgow International Exhibition 9, 12
gloves 30, 77–81
Gobelin stitch 99
Golding, Arthur 135
Graham, James 125
Great Fire of London 25
Great Seal 126, 128–131
Griffiths, Percival D. 93
Guild of Embroiderers 17

Ham House, The Stapleton Collection 23
Hamlet 30
handkerchief 51, 52
Harold II 83

145

Harrison, Edmund 17
Hastings, Henry 100
Henrietta Maria 17
Henry IV of France 21
Henry IV, part 2 27
Henry VII 51, 60
Henry VIII 15, 83, 124
Heriot, George 87, 88
Home, Elizabeth 74, 75
hood 83, 90, 93, 95
Hopton, Sir Ralph 111
Howard, Elizabeth 67, 69
Howard, Henry 97
Huguenots 21, 135
Hunt, John 108
Hutton Castle 11, 134
Hyde, Bridget 24

Incorporation of Tailors 17
indigo 54, 55
Irwin Untermyer Collection 49
Isabella, Queen of Castile 124
Islam, Sir Thomas 109

James VI and I 12, 15, 17, 25, 27, 28, 60, 67, 72, 73, 87, 91, 92, 118
James VII and II 25
Janssens van Ceulen, Cornelius 19, 20, 21
Jesus Christ 60, 124
Jones, Inigo 17

Kenwood House (Suffolk Collection) 17, 65, 69, 74, 78
kermes 68
Kilbryde Castle, Perthshire 119
King Midas 134, 135
knitting 105–108
Kunsthistorisches Museum, Vienna 62
Kyoto Costume Institute 102

lace 6, 9, 15, 19, 20, 21, 23, 25, 63, 65, 77, 79, 97, 120, 137
Lady Lever Art Gallery 12, 119
Langport, Battle of 111, 118
Larkin, William 15, 17, 62, 65, 77, 78
Law Castle, Kilbride 126
Layton, Frances 62
Layton, Margaret 62, 63
le Moyne des Morgues, Jacques 38, 53
Lee, William 105
Leslie, Sir David 125

Lever, William Hesketh 12, 119
Levett, Catherine 71
Levett, Reverend Richard 71
Levett, Sir Richard 71
Levett, William 10, 71
Levey, Santina 68
Lockey, Rowland 91, 92
Lombards 30
London 15, 17, 19, 25, 27, 28, 38, 44, 52, 62, 65, 67, 71, 74, 77, 78, 83, 87, 91, 102, 105, 108, 109, 116, 123, 129, 130
long-and-short stitch 70, 81
Louis XIV 21, 134, 136
lure 88, 89, 91
Lyon 31

Manchester Gallery of Costume 99, 119
Markham, Gervaise 98
Mary II 25
Mary, Queen of Scots 67, 68
Massey, Sir Edward 118
Master, James 117
metalwork 11
Metamorphoses 135
Metropolitan Museum of Art, New York 49
Montagu, Sir Charles 129
Montgomery, Lieutenant-General Robert 125
Moryson, Fynes 41
Monck, General George 125
Mytens, Daniel 67, 69

Naples 105
Naseby, Battle of 118
National Gallery 83, 116
National Portrait Gallery 19, 24, 28, 52, 91, 112, 130
nightcaps 12, 27, 28, 29, 31–35, 111–114, 117, 121, 126
North, Francis 93, 129, 130, 131
North, Lord Dudley 92, 93, 129
Norton, John (5th Baron of Grantley) 80

Oes 49, 97
Ophelia 30
or nué 15
Ottoman Empire 120, 123
Overton, John 31

Paris 31
Partridge, Frank 43

passing 41, 70, 86
Pepys, Samuel 21, 80, 117, 126
Pett, Phineas 28, 29
petticoat 10, 21, 24, 63, 65, 67–76, 136
Philiphaugh, Battle of 125
plaited braid stitch 29, 35, 41, 45, 61, 62, 71, 102, 141
Plymouth 25
Pope, Frances 129
Pope, Thomas (of Wroxton) 129
Pope, Sir William 92, 93
pouch 85, 86, 94
Poyntz, Adrian 31
Protestant 15, 21, 135
punto in aria 65
Puritans 19, 120
purl 84, 101, 105

Radclyffe, Frances 30
Reformation 15
Restoration 21, 25, 117, 118, 123, 125–131
reticella 63, 65
Richard II 83
rinceau 29, 30, 31, 38, 41, 44, 49, 51, 55, 58, 61, 67, 102
rococo stitch 103
Rose, John 23
running stitch 38, 51, 53, 108, 115

Sackville, Edward 15, 17
Sackville, Richard 77, 78
satin stitch 70, 81, 119, 133
Scottish National Portrait Gallery 112
Scougall, John 87
Seymour, Frances 32
Shakespeare, William 17, 25, 27, 30, 32, 55, 135
Shorleyker, Richard 31
Sibmacher, Johann 68
silver-gilt 17, 29, 35, 41, 44, 45, 47, 51, 52, 53, 58, 61, 63, 79, 80, 81, 84, 90, 91, 93, 102, 107, 108, 112, 113, 123, 129
slippers 111, 114, 117
spangles 41, 45, 49, 52, 53, 55, 57, 60, 61, 63, 67, 75, 79, 80, 97, 113, 119, 123, 129
Spain 51, 68, 105, 124
split stitch 15, 33, 133
St George's Chapel, Windsor Castle 71

St John's College, Cambridge 129
St Paul 37
stem stitch 33, 38, 45, 53, 133
stomacher 11, 24, 133, 134
Stent, Peter 31
Stuart, Arbella 73
Stuart, Princess Elizabeth 75
Stuart, Mary (Queen of Scots) 67, 68
Sultan Murad III 123
Swain, Margaret 67, 68
sweet bag 97–102
Sydney, Madame 39

Talbot, Elizabeth 30
Talbot, Gilbert (Earl of Shrewsbury) 73
tapestries 11, 12, 39, 83, 85, 88
tent stitch 99, 101
Throckmorton, Mary 51, 52

Trevelyon, Thomas 31, 32
Tudor, Arthur 51
Turner, William 34

Union of the Crowns 15, 125
Untermyer, Judge Irwin 12

van Dyck, Sir Anthony 71, 116, 117
van Somer, Paul 87
Veel, Colonel Thomas (of Alverstone) 111, 117, 118
Veel, Nicholas 117
Venice 68
vest 21, 23, 24, 117
Veth, Cornelia 20, 21
Victoria and Albert Museum 7, 44, 63, 102, 103, 108, 109, 114, 117, 123
Villiers, Charles 116
Vinciolo, Federigo 31

Virgin Mary 53, 60
Vyner, Lady Mary 24
Vyner, Sir Robert 24

waistcoat 23, 51, 52, 55, 57–66, 67, 69, 71, 105–110, 111, 114, 117, 136
Walsingham, Frances 102
Warner, William Lee 71
Wars of the Three Kingdoms 111
Westminster 21
wheel farthingales 17
William III 25
woad 54
woven wheel stitch 33, 45, 52, 58
Wright, John Michael 21, 22, 24
Wroxton Abbey 92, 129

Yale Center for British Art 22
York, Elizabeth of 60